RSYA

OCT 2001

Babysitting

Babysitting
Revised Edition

by FRANCES S. DAYEE

Franklin Watts
A Division of Grolier Publishing
New York * London * Hong Kong * Sydney
Danbury, Connecticut

This book is dedicated to all children, parents, and sitters—especially those in my family—who shared their experiences to make this book a reality. Also, I want to thank Dr. Jeffrey Lindenbaum.

Visit Franklin Watts on the Internet at:
http://publishing.grolier.com

Cartoons by Heidi Graf
Book design by Vicki Fischman

Library of Congress Cataloging-in-Publication Data

Dayee, Frances S.
    Babysitting / by Frances S. Dayee.—Rev. ed.
        p. cm.
    Includes bibliographical references and index.
    Summary: A guide to earning money as a babysitter, with advice on getting customers, safety, and handling emergencies.
        ISBN 0-531-11745-6 0-531-16520-5 (pbk.)
        1. Babysitting—Vocational guidance—United States—Juvenile literature.
    [1. Babysitting—Handbooks, manuals, etc. 2. Babysitters.] I. Title.
HQ769.5 .D39 2000
649'.1'0248—dc21
                                                                        99-087945

✳ Contents ✳

✳ Introduction ✳

It has been a decade since the first edition of *Babysitting* was published. This second edition includes several new components and more current information.

For this book, I interviewed many babysitters, parents, and children. Their experiences will help you succeed. Excellent babysitters don't always do everything right, but they learn from their mistakes and those of others.

I've added three new chapters: "Meals and Snacks," "First Aid," and "Accidents and Emergencies." "Meals and Snacks" includes information on handling breast milk and baby formula and discusses food allergies and the importance of asking parents for their guidelines concerning proper foods and mealtime rules.

"First Aid" addresses minor problems. Of course, taking a first-aid class is the best preparation. Some important components of this chapter are the list of emergencies that require calling for help *before* calling the parent, a list of common household poisons, a condensed list of common first-aid problems with guidelines for early treatment, and a sample emergency-consent form.

Like "First Aid," "Accidents and Emergencies" does not cover everything. A large volume could be written on the subject and some topics would still be omitted. Statistics show that 95 percent of all child-related accidents can be prevented. Awareness is the watchword. People can prepare for only some emergencies. I've included a few tips on how to handle some common emergencies.

Other chapters have new elements, such as information on how to deal with divorced parents and their children. There are new illustrations, chapter checklists for quick reference, and an updated "To Find Out More" section that includes books, videos, and online sites.

Although information is important, experience ultimately provides the good judgment that produces a babysitting expert. Be proud as you gain experience, for babysitting is a noble profession.

—*Frances Dayee*

Babysitting

✳ Chapter One ✳

Beginnings

Y ou are *babysitting* for three-year-old Dan and four-month-old Heather. While Heather naps in her bouncy seat, you make Dan a peanut-butter-and-jelly sandwich for his lunch. He climbs up on a chair to sit at the kitchen table and eat. Then Heather starts to cry. It's time to feed and change her.

You decide to organize everything before you get her. You warm a bottle and mix cereal in a bowl. You gather up clean clothes and a diaper, stack them on the bathroom counter, and lay out the diapering pad. Then, on your way to get Heather, the telephone rings.

The caller wants to talk to Dan's mother. You let the person know that Mrs. Delbert is busy and can't come to the phone right now, but if the person will leave her name and number, Mrs. Delbert will get back to her as soon as she can. You write the information on the phone-message board, hang up the phone, and turn around just in time to see Dan holding Heather upside down. "*Baby* crying," he says.

What should you do?

  a) Rush over and grab Heather.
  b) Yell, "How did you get that baby?"
  c) Talk quietly to Dan.
  d) Panic.

The best answer is *c*. Tell Dan how lucky Heather is to have a big brother like him. Smile reassuringly at him as you walk toward him to take the baby.

Once Heather is secure in your arms, tell Dan how much you appreciated his concern for his sister. Tell him you know that he wanted to help. Ask him if he would please come and get you the next time, however, rather than get Heather by himself. Don't be afraid to admit that you probably took a very long time getting to his sister. Even a short time seems long to young children.

Keep a Cool Head

Fourteen-year-old Anthony has been babysitting for two years. Early in his sitting career, Anthony wouldn't have had the slightest idea what to do in the situation described above. Maybe even now, as a *savvy* sitter, he wouldn't know exactly what to do. But his advice would be, "Keep a cool head," because certainly panicking doesn't work. Thanks to experience, Anthony knows better now.

"Once when I was changing a baby's cloth diaper, he started screaming. I thought I had stuck him with a pin, and he was bleeding to death. I was going to call the neighbors, the paramedics, my mom, and the doctor.

"I hadn't stuck him. I probably pinched him," Anthony admits. "But I scared myself so badly that I scared him and his brother. They both started to cry. I finally had to call my mom to find out how to get the kids to stop crying."

Since Anthony realizes that his fear scared the children, he'd also be able to figure out that rushing over to the baby and yelling at Dan would not be good choices. If he rushed up to Dan and tried to grab Heather, the *toddler* might drop the baby. If he yelled and scared Dan, the same thing might happen.

One Babysitter's Experience

No one can predict what his or her babysitting career is going to be like, but this is how LeVelle began.

LeVelle's eyes light up to match her smile. "My babysitting career started the summer I was ten. I was hired as a mother's helper for an eighteen-month-old child." The mother, an author, wanted someone to play with her daughter while she wrote.

"Before I ever watched Yolanda, I went to the gym with her and her mother several times. Her mother thought it would be a good way for me to get to know her."

LeVelle babysat for Yolanda for several years. "As Yolanda grew older, we read books—lots and lots and lots of books. When we weren't reading books, we played with her puppet theater or pretended. We played babysitter a lot, and she was the babysitter. Then I'd act just like her and she'd say, 'Girls are supposed to be nice,' and I'd say, 'Is that right? I didn't know that.'"

LeVelle, now a senior in high school, has an afternoon job in a dentist's office. She still babysits in the evenings though because, "They love me. All the children I babysit for love me, and I love them."

The First Sitter

It's amazing how many beginnings there are in the world. The first significant one for you was the day you were born. It was also a beginning for your parents. At that moment, their world grew to include you. To many parents, their child is more important than life itself. If you understand this bond, you might begin to understand why parents can be difficult to work for. It might help you to remember that parents learn every day, just like everyone else. That bit of common sense may seem unbelievable to you, but it's true.

One parent shared this insight: "When I started hiring babysitters, I really wasn't sure what I wanted in a sitter. That's why I wanted to visit Kristen and Joy in their home before I hired them.

"Family values, being careful, taking the job seriously—those things are very important. I felt they would relate to my child well because they came from a large family. They were children who were used to being around other children. I liked that. There's so much of it that's gut reaction that it's hard to analyze."

Babysitter's Parents

Parents focus much of their energy on teaching their children to be independent. At the same time, they don't want to see their children grow up too soon, so they also put a lot of energy into keeping them from becoming too independent too quickly. Parents know that everyone makes mistakes in life, but they want to save their children from making them.

Your parents probably keep wondering if they gave you all the skills necessary to succeed in life. You'd be surprised at how proud your parents are as they watch you jump the hurdles of life and hear of your successes. They also face those beginnings, but in a different way.

One parent notes, "When Renato first started babysitting, I worried. After all, he's just a kid, and look at all the things that can happen. When the compliments from his customers on having such a wonderful, responsible, conscientious son started pouring in, I stopped worrying. It made me look at my son in a new way."

Your parents will look at you in a new way too. But they are still your parents, and they might have a difficult time letting go as you begin babysitting. If you need them for support, though, let them know. Remember that babysitting is a new beginning for you and your parents. It is also a new beginning for the people you babysit for— your clients.

Positive Beginnings

Carol was going to babysit for Dean, a six-year-old whose parents had divorced. Dean greeted her by announcing, "I'm not a baby!" Later, though, when she left, Dean sang a different tune. "Carol can babysit me any time she wants," he told his dad.

What made the difference was that Carol thought ahead. She brought a game of wooden stack blocks to play with Dean. They built a tower of blocks, removing one block at a time and trying not to cause the tower to fall.

The person who made it fall lost the game. Neither Dean nor Carol kept track of who won or lost, though. They just giggled and laughed when the tower swayed or fell and gathered the blocks to play again. Dean couldn't stop talking about what fun he'd had, and Carol had initiated a terrific beginning with him.

Not every first experience with a child will be as wonderful as Carol's experience with Dean. But you can begin any babysitter-child relationship on a positive note by anticipating the child's needs and planning a fun, age-appropriate activity.

Chapter Checklist

✓ Remain calm—children reflect your reactions.

✓ Babysitting is a new beginning for you, your parents, and the people you babysit for.

✓ If you need your parents' support, let them know.

✓ You can begin any babysitter-child relationship on a positive note by anticipating the child's needs and planning a fun, age-appropriate activity.

Chapter Two

A Profession

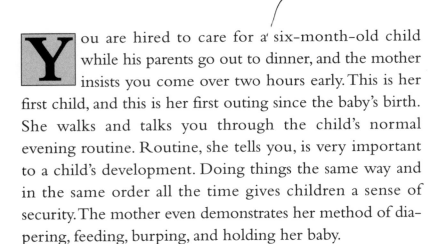

You are hired to care for a six-month-old child while his parents go out to dinner, and the mother insists you come over two hours early. This is her first child, and this is her first outing since the baby's birth. She walks and talks you through the child's normal evening routine. Routine, she tells you, is very important to a child's development. Doing things the same way and in the same order all the time gives children a sense of security. The mother even demonstrates her method of diapering, feeding, burping, and holding her baby.

You conclude that you cannot live up to this woman's expectations, so you:

   a) refuse to babysit
   b) explain that you will be happy to babysit, but you can't promise to do everything exactly as she does

c) tell her that you will do what she wants—and then do everything your way

d) try to follow the routine, but don't worry if things get out of order as long as the baby is happy

e) babysit once, and see how it goes

There are four acceptable answers. The only one that is not acceptable is *c.* As a babysitter, it is your responsibility to follow directions to the best of your ability. But if what the mother expects is unreasonable, the best alternative is to refuse to work for her. This option is preferable to pretending to do things the parent's way.

Tera was three months old when Phyllis, a single parent, went back to work. "I had the sitter come over a couple of days ahead of time," Phyllis says. "I spent hours showing her exactly how I took care of Tera."

Looking back, Phyllis says she can see how foolish she was. "I was lucky my sitter didn't quit. After a while I settled down. Tera was happy. That made me happy." Did the sitter do everything her way? "No, but she tried."

You can be proud of babysitting. Good babysitters are trustworthy; they know how to follow directions; they have experience in getting along with people of all ages; and they are reliable.

Babysitting Is an Active Job

The word "babysitting" is misleading. Taking care of babies is the exception rather than the rule. And sitting is the last position in which parents or their children want to see their child's caregiver.

"It's important to me that the babysitter play with my daughter and interact with her," says Ms. Doyle. "One of the good things about Dana's opportunity to be with a babysitter is that a young person is more likely to play with Dana rather than just watch her play. I play with Dana as much as I can, but children can play with children in a way that adults can't just by the nature and proximity of their ages.

"I'm interested in active interaction rather than passive, and it's important to me that there's some initiative in the interactive play experience. One of my best babysitters brings her favorite books, games, and toys from home to share. She makes an effort to plan fun activities."

Most parents prefer sitters who play with their children, and many babysitters enjoy their work more when they're busy. When William began his career as a sitter, he was passive and self-centered. He learned that these attitudes don't work in babysitting.

"When I first started babysitting," William says, "I just went to the house, put the baby to sleep, and did my homework or amused myself in some way. As I got more jobs, I began to realize it was more fun to play with the baby. Also, the parents like it better. And you get return business if the child likes you." William's insight helped him to become an active, child-focused sitter.

One parent remarked, "I hire someone who is interested in my children, who does things with them. I don't want someone who is just interested in making money and hanging out." As with any job, the more you put into babysitting, the more you get out of it.

Know Yourself

Before you begin to babysit, ask yourself whether you like children. Think about whether you get along with your sisters and brothers (if you have any). Ask yourself if you know how to make children feel better when they are upset, and if you enjoy playing with little ones. Consider how you might react if they irritate you.

If you wrinkled your nose at the words "sisters" and "brothers," it doesn't mean that you don't like children. Your sisters and brothers live with you and know just how to bug you. That's why sitting for your own *siblings* can be one of the hardest babysitting jobs. Having younger sisters and brothers does not automatically qualify you as a babysitter, of course. Many sitters who are only children (or the youngest child) make excellent babysitters. However, the reason they are good babysitters is that they like children.

The best way to find out if you like children is to spend time with them. Park and recreation centers are often looking for volunteers to help with small children. Call day-care facilities and ask if they need a volunteer. Many schools have extended day-care programs for students. Inquire at a school in your neighborhood. Check churches or synagogues in your neighborhood to see if they provide babysitting during services. Being around children will help you find out what age group you are most comfortable with.

Eighteen-year-old Joseph confessed, "I like little kids, not big kids. I babysat for some [older] kids who were perfect angels while their parents were home. When the parents left, they were hyper little brats. I worried the whole time that they were going to get hurt, but I couldn't control them. I didn't go back." After that experience, Joseph was careful to ask the ages of the children before he accepted a job.

Bette thought she'd prefer babies. After taking care of a few infants, she realized that she became impatient when she didn't know why the infant was crying. People had told her that she'd recognize the different cries a baby makes, but when she couldn't tell the cries apart, she felt inadequate. Now she knows the age group she prefers: "Kids who talk. They can tell me what they like and don't like, what they want and don't want. Baby detective work is not for me."

William discovered, over time, that his favorite age for a child is one-and-a-half to two. "They like you just the way you are," he says. "No peer pressure. It's great!" If you know the age group you prefer to care for, success usually follows.

Volunteer Babysitting Pays Off

Volunteer babysitting provides several benefits. First, it allows you to find out whether you like working with youngsters and what age groups you prefer. Second, when you are asked if you have babysitting experience, you can say, "Yes." Third, volunteering your time shows that you are a responsible, giving person. If you discover that you love babysitting, you'll know it is worth pursuing. A volunteer job may even become a paid position. Discovering that you enjoy working with children might eventually lead you to become a teacher! On the other hand, if you find that you don't really like being around children, you'll know that babysitting is not for you.

Volunteering shows interest. Volunteers don't stick around if they don't enjoy the work. If you're a good volunteer babysitter, people will notice. Don't be shy about requesting a letter of recommendation when you're applying for a paid position. A letter of recommendation makes a good impression.

Babysitting Classes

Another way to impress potential clients and develop competence is to take a babysitting class. Few courses give potential sitters an opportunity to work with children, but most courses provide valuable background information—especially if you are inexperienced.

When Glenn decided not to take a class, he realized that babysitting was not for him. He says, "My parents want me to take a class on how to save a life and everything before I babysit. I think it's a good idea, but I don't have enough interest in babysitting to want to take classes."

Babysitting takes commitment. If you don't have enough interest, it's better not to babysit. If you're interested in taking a babysitting class, try calling a boys' or girls' club, a city park and recreation center, your local library, or a hospital. Ask what and where courses are being offered.

Some organizations specialize in teaching babysitting courses. For instance, Campfire Boys and Girls offer a Special Sitters class that focuses on caring for developmentally delayed and disabled children. Red Cross babysitting classes focus on decision-making, safety, and first aid. Safe Sitter, a not-for-profit group, offers seminars for boys and girls aged eleven to thirteen on the basics of sitting, plus rescue techniques and how to handle choking.

By contacting the organization teaching the course, you will discover if you're interested in the training that they offer. At the same time, you can find out where classes are held, when they start, how to sign up, and how much they cost. A sitter class is a giant first step to becoming a professional.

Chapter Checklist

✓ As an employee, it is your responsibility to follow directions to the best of your ability.

✓ As with any job, the more you put into babysitting, the more you get out of it.

✓ Before you begin to babysit, ask yourself whether you like children.

✓ Sitting for your own siblings can be one of the hardest babysitting jobs.

✓ Volunteer babysitting provides several benefits.

✓ If you know the age group you prefer to care for, success usually follows.

✓ Babysitting takes commitment. If you don't have enough interest, it's better not to babysit.

✓ Impress potential clients and develop competence by taking a babysitting class.

Another way to find a babysitting job is to talk to your sitter friends. Ask them to recommend you the next time they get a job offer that they can't accept. A good babysitter is usually in demand.

Even when people seem safe and familiar, it doesn't hurt to have potential clients screened by an adult. The most logical screeners are people who love you, who are concerned about your welfare, and who are more experienced in the ways of the world.

When Jill took her babysitting class at a local recreation center, she was placed on a babysitter referral list. "Before my parents would allow my name to be put on the list, they made me promise to let them talk to referred clients before I did," she said. "I didn't mind. After all, there was no way we could know everyone who came to the rec center. It made me feel safer."

Marie felt safe when she answered an ad in her church bulletin. The job was for an after-school day-care person in the parish school. Marie wrote a resumé that listed jobs she had held and gave character references. She wore her best clothes and a smile for the interview. Before she left the interview, she was told that even if she didn't get the job, they wanted her to know she had done an excellent job of preparing for the interview.

Andy doesn't have to worry about interviews. He gets his jobs just by being one in a long line of highly qualified sister and brother babysitters. But keeping those jobs in the family depends on him. Andy is also lucky because his parents already know his clients. Parents feel less comfortable when you babysit for strangers. And, yes, you do have to deal with your parents.

Mr. Kirby wants to meet his daughter's potential clients in advance. "I can tell a lot about a family when I walk into the house. There is a warmth or coldness about the place, and I'm not talking about the heat." If, for some reason, Mr. Kirby can't meet the family, he wants to know how they found out that his daughter babysits. That information tells him a lot about the family too. "I don't always interfere in my daughter's business, but I feel I have a right to put my two cents in. After all, it's her safety I'm concerned about."

Before You Get the Job

Before a babysitting interview, you need to know what your parents expect of you. One mother of a babysitter puts it this way:

> *My son is required to check with his father or me before he accepts a job. We want to be sure there is nothing on the calendar that interferes with his responsibility or commitment to family. He has to write down the person's name and phone number so that I can reach him. During the week, he is supposed to be home by 9:00 P.M. If he is scheduled to babysit until 9:00, and the couple gets home at 9:30, that may be okay. But if that couple keeps him late on a regular basis, he may have to tell them that he can't babysit for them anymore. On weekends, my son may babysit until 12:30 A.M. or, if it's someone we know, we'll talk things over and certain arrangements can be made.*

Many an argument between parents and their babysitting teenagers has been caused by a misunderstanding in expectations. Talk things over in advance with your parents. This *strategy* doesn't guarantee smooth sailing all the time—unexpected, unexplored situations may still arise. But, on the whole, it pays to try to work your jobs around and within parental schedules, guidelines, and expectations.

Decide on a place to keep the names, addresses, and phone numbers of your clients for easy reference. One parent said, "We have a book. If it's not in the book, they don't go."

Another parent pointed to a large wall calendar. "Everything that my daughter schedules goes on this calendar. Whether she schedules it or I schedule it, everything is written down so that I know exactly where she is. Sometimes she calls to say, 'If I'm gone, I'm at the park with the children,' so I know what's going on. No matter where she is, I know."

When one young adult babysat, she found it a definite advantage to be able to locate her mother. "Mom lets me know where to reach her if she's not going to be home. One time, I called her at my grandmother's because the toilet was plugged up and I couldn't find the plunger. She suggested places to look that never occurred to me. Getting in touch with her saved the day."

If you're from a family of babysitters, you have an advantage because your parents are already trained to some extent. On the other hand, they might need your services at home. One mother states, "I realize that's how Helen makes her money, but she has to be here when I need her. She figures I'm the one who got myself into this situation [all those little ones running around]. Why should she have any responsibility? I see her point, and I try not to take advantage of her, but home and family are always first."

If things aren't perfect, be willing to compromise. Sometimes the excitement of being an independent business person and building up a cash flow overcomes good sense. Even if you are not responsible for chores around the house, you need to plan time for homework, social life, and sleep. A person who is not well rested or is stressed by lack of time for friends and homework does not do well with children. In fact, parents often say that stress is the main reason they want to take a break from their children. Just as parents need the time away to relax and refresh themselves, you need time for yourself too. Try to balance babysitting with your personal activities.

Chapter Checklist

✓ When searching for a job, consider your safety.

✓ Discuss safe, effective ways to advertise your services with your parents or another responsible adult.

✓ Consider letting your parents screen prospective clients not known to the family.

✓ It pays to plan sitting jobs within parental schedules, guidelines, and expectations.

✓ Create a method of making the name, address, and phone number of your client available to your parents.

✓ Try to balance babysitting with your personal activities.

Chapter Four

How Much to Charge

Most babysitters have an idea what they would like to be paid, but they are uncomfortable talking about money with adults. In 1964, the going rate for a babysitter was fifty cents an hour. Today, that rate sounds insane! There is no right way to decide what to charge, but here are some ideas:

    a) let clients set your fee
    b) ask experienced babysitters what they charge
    c) ask several parents what they are willing to pay
    d) ask family members for advice

Some parents prefer not to set the fee. One parent said, "I really like a babysitter to tell me what he or she expects to be paid, and not to say, 'I don't know' or 'I don't care.'"

Many people try to get the least expensive sitter because admission to any event and dining out, plus a babysitting fee, can break the bank for some parents.

Mr. and Mrs. Lowell have two sets of twins, sixteen months apart. "I need someone who is willing to take a reasonable rate of pay," says Mrs. Lowell, "or we can't go out. I think sitters should be willing to understand the financial needs of the family they are sitting for."

Krista admits she is willing to take a job for less money "when I don't do anything but play with the kids. But it's hard to find kids that good, and I charge more for kids who are difficult to handle."

Roberto, an experienced sitter, charges a base price per hour for one child, doubles it for two children, and then adds fifty cents per hour for each additional child. But he remembers the time when he took what he could get. "With experience, my clients raised my pay. Then I charged the higher fee to new customers." A good babysitter is definitely a treasure, so don't sell yourself short and undercharge. Expect fair payment while charging a fair price.

Babysitting rates may differ by fifty cents to a dollar per hour from one part of town to another. Do some detective work. What do your friends charge? What does your sister or brother charge? What do babysitting instructors suggest as the going rate? Talk to your teachers. Ask them what they think. Many of them have children, so they will know firsthand. Call people who have children. Ask them what they pay and what they think is fair. Experience counts. Classes in first aid, *CPR*, and babysitting can also help you get a higher rate.

Good Qualities = Higher Pay

Mrs. Myron says, "I think babysitters should be paid well and I think they should feel good about that. I'll pay anything they are charging if they're good."

Mrs. Myron admits the key word is *good*. Parents often describe a good sitter as someone with these characteristics:

- dependable—uses common sense and considers safety important
- reliable—can be trusted to follow directions and family rules
- interested in and enjoys children
- respectful of family privacy—doesn't snoop or gossip
- good role model
- honest, truthful, and trustworthy
- calm
- actively involved with child/children
- serious about the job—arrives on time
- kind, gentle, friendly, and forgiving

It's obvious that if you want repeat business, you must please the parents. But, if you think they are the only ones you need to please, think again.

Mrs. Carla, a mother of two said, "This one girl would come and babysit, and my kitchen would always be cleaner than when I left it, sparkling, but my kids weren't happy with her at all. They said that when she wasn't cleaning, she was watching television. She doesn't babysit for me anymore. Another girl—who only sat for me once—made my kids stay in their bedroom the whole time while she talked on the phone."

It pays to remember that children tell their parents how they feel about the babysitter. Here are some comments from children who liked their babysitter.

A good sitter:

- likes me.
- does things with me.
- listens to me when I talk.
- respects my privacy.
- talks to me instead of talking on the phone.
- doesn't make fun of me.
- makes me feel safe.
- isn't bossy.
- acts silly sometimes.
- doesn't yell.

Most people value these qualities in their friends and loved ones, so it's easy to see why compliments from the children in your care might add to your worth as a babysitter. When determining your fee, consider whether you have the qualities that parents and children value in a good sitter.

Decisions, Decisions

After you decide what to charge, be very clear when you discuss your fee with your clients. Before you begin, write a script for yourself that also includes any points you feel are important. For instance, are you willing to take checks or do you want them to pay you in cash? When do you expect to get paid? Usually, you will want to be paid the day you babysit. If you're sitting twice a week, it may be acceptable to be paid on the last day of each week. Do you charge more after midnight? If so, how much more? Bring up these points the first time you talk to a potential client.

Make sure that the script you have written feels comfortable to you. Prepare responses in case the client wants to negotiate your fee. Under what circumstances is payment by check acceptable? If the client questions your fee, explain what you base your fee on. If there is still a difference of opinion, you have three choices.

The first choice is to refuse the job and hope someone else will be willing to pay your rate. The second choice is to negotiate a compromise. If your client offers you $1 an hour less than you asked for, request an amount between both rates. The third choice is to accept a lower rate. Taking less money from one customer doesn't mean that you can't charge another customer what you believe you deserve.

In fact, there are occasions when taking less is the smart thing to do. Lowering your price to meet others' needs may create more business. Happy customers brag about their babysitters. Also, when customers feel they are getting a bargain, they'll call you more often.

There's an old saying, "A bird in the hand is worth two in the bush." It means that sometimes it's better to take what you are offered rather than wait around for what you might get. Weigh the advantages and disadvantages of taking less money. Sometimes a lower-paying customer makes up for it by leaving a special snack for you in the kitchen or remembering you on birthdays and holidays.

Keeping Records

When you have a business, it's very important to keep accurate records. The first thing you need is a personal calendar with room to write information for each day. Enter the following potential schedule conflicts: medical appointments, practice sessions, personal recreation time, study sessions (don't ever assume that you will have time to study for an important test while babysitting), extracurricular activities, lessons, and family commitments. Next, check with your family to find out if there are any other dates that need to be blocked out.

Keep the calendar close to where you will take your business calls so that you can see at a glance if the time you are needed as a sitter is open. Update your calendar with your family on a regular basis.

Keep a note pad and pencil near the phone. Write new client information on the notepad. Ask for the correct spelling of the client's name. If the name is pronounced differently than it's spelled, write it phonetically so that you can pronounce it correctly the next time you talk to this person. Always verify the spelling of names. To insure that your information is correct, read back the address and phone number and confirm the date and time you are to sit.

Gordon says that one time he wrote his client's information on the wrong date and was at a ball game when they came to pick him up. He was lucky that he had a babysitting sister to take over for him or he could have lost that customer.

When you are certain the information is correct, carefully transfer it to your calendar. It is also helpful to keep a separate record of your customers. One sitter keeps a record of clients on his computer. He includes each client's name, address, and phone number; how much he charges that customer; the names and ages of the children; and other relevant information, such as when he's supposed to babysit and whether the children have allergies. Index cards and a card file also work well for keeping records.

Paying Taxes

Last but not least, check with state and county tax offices and the Internal Revenue Service to see whether you need to pay taxes. The laws for federal income tax are different from state and county tax laws—and can be very complicated. To be on the safe side, check with all three agencies to see if you must pay taxes. If taxes are to be subtracted from your income, you'll probably want to charge a higher rate.

If you need to pay taxes, record your business earnings and expenses for accounting purposes. Any kind of spreadsheet or notebook will do. Enter the date and how much you earned in your record book as soon as you get home from a job so that you don't forget them. Anything you buy that is directly related to your babysitting business—such as this book, the cost of babysitting classes, and printed flyers or business cards—is a business expense. Keep sales slips and receipts for any business expense as proof of purchase. Enter all expenses in your record book, along with the date that they were paid, in case you are eligible for tax deductions.

Chapter Checklist

✓ To decide what to charge, do some research.

✓ Expect fair payment while charging a fair price.

✓ When determining your fee, consider whether you have the qualities that parents and children value in a sitter.

✓ Prepare responses in case the client wants to negotiate your fee.

✓ Weigh the advantages and disadvantages of taking less money.

✓ Keep good records, and enter potential schedule conflicts on your calendar.

✓ Consider keeping a record on each customer, recording relevant information.

✓ Check with state and county tax offices and the Internal Revenue Service to see whether you need to pay taxes.

✓ If you need to pay taxes, record your business earnings and expenses for accounting purposes.

Chapter Five

Interviewing

A lthough most employment interviews are face-to-face meetings, babysitting interviews usually take place over the phone and may seem to be more like an interrogation than a discussion. Try to relax, and feel free to politely ask for all the information you feel you need.

Interviews can be unsettling, so preparing for an interview gives you more confidence. One way to prepare is to interview yourself in the mirror or have a friend play the role of a prospective client. Answering questions aloud helps you decide whether the response is what you want to say, the way you want to say it. Taking time to practice smoothes out the rough spots and makes you more comfortable. When you're comfortable, you can be yourself. And being yourself is the best person you can be.

Another way to prepare for an interview is to anticipate the questions a prospective client is likely to ask (just as you do when your prepare for a test at school). Then write and practice your responses. A parent may want to know what experience you've had; the names of some people who would give you a good recommendation; and how much you charge. If you haven't had any experience, be honest, but also tell the caller why you would make a good babysitter. Suggest the names of people who would be glad to supply a character reference. Good sources are a teacher, a neighbor, one of your parents' friends, or one of your friend's parents. It's always wise to ask people in advance if you may use them as a reference. Then they have time to think about all your good qualities.

While preparing for an interview, remember to think about your safety. If you don't know the family, say you will get back to them after you talk to your parents. This strategy gives you and your parents time to be sure the job is safe. If you are still unsure, you and your parents can arrange a visit with the client. Consider other risks, too, such as walking home alone after dark.

Discussion Topics for Interviews

Think about questions and personal guidelines you wish to discuss with a client during a phone or face-to-face interview. How do you feel about babysitting for children who are ill? How do your parents feel? If you talk to your parents and they decide they do not want you to sit for a child who has a contagious illness, it's fair to establish an "I don't babysit children who are contagious" guideline. Neither schools nor day-care facilities want sick children to attend because sickness spreads. Your health and the health of your family are important. Of course, that goes both ways. If you are ill, don't spread your germs to another family. Call to cancel as soon as you can so that your client can make other arrangements. If you have a list of babysitting friends, ask their permission to share their names and phone numbers with your client in case you need a backup.

If clients cancel at the last minute, you might want to set a cancellation fee. One young adult charges a fee only if she had turned down another job, but most professionals—from hairstylists to physicians—charge a fee for broken appointments without twenty-four hours' notice. If your policy is to charge a cancellation fee, it's important to notify your client during the interview—before cancellations occur.

An interview is also the best time to ask if the child takes any medication on a regular basis or has any special medical problems. Does the child take the medication willingly? If you are going to be required to dispense medication, ask for written instructions.

Some medical conditions, such as *seizures*, are controlled by medication. But if the prospect of a seizure frightens you, don't be afraid to turn down the job. Ask yourself whether you would feel comfortable caring for a child with special medical problems, such as *asthma*, *diabetes*, or *hemophilia*. If someone in your family has one of these conditions, it may not bother you at all to sit with children who suffer from that disorder. If you are not familiar with such disorders, their symptoms, and their treatments, you can get information about them from the library, your doctor, and the child's parents. Most people know whether they would remain calm in a medical emergency or freeze with fear. Use that knowledge as the basis for your decision.

❋ SAMPLE PHONE INTERVIEW ❋

Prospective Client: Hello. This is Bob Jordan. Is Rachel in?

Babysitter: This is Rachel.

Prospective Client: The apartment complex manager gave me your flyer. How old are you, and how much babysitting experience do you have?

Babysitter: I'm thirteen and I'm just starting my business, Mr. Jordan. But I've taken babysitting classes, which included CPR, and I have first-aid training. I really like kids.

Prospective Client: Sounds like you do, and the manager gave you a good recommendation. My wife and I need someone to watch Doug from five o'clock to eleven on Saturday.

Babysitter: I'm available to babysit on Saturday night. How old is Doug, and where would I babysit?

Prospective Client: Doug is three. We're in apartment 4D.

Babysitter: I have to check with my parents before I schedule new families, but let me see if I have all your information correct. You need a sitter on Saturday from five in the evening to approximately eleven. You're in apartment 4D. And do you spell your last name J o r d a n ?

Prospective Client: That's correct.

Babysitter: Mr. Jordan, when I sit I charge $_____ an hour until midnight. After midnight, my fee goes up to $_____ an hour. I expect to be paid in cash the evening I sit.

Prospective Client: That sounds reasonable.

Babysitter: Does Doug have any medical problems or food allergies that I need to be aware of?

Prospective Client: No. He has an ear infection, but he's been on medication for more than twenty-four hours—so he's not contagious.

Babysitter: Will I be giving Doug his medication?

Prospective Client: No, we'll take care of that before we leave.

Babysitter: Will I be expected to feed Doug, and what time does he go to bed?

Prospective Client: He usually eats around five, but we will have the meal all ready for you. Please plan on eating with Doug since he eats better when he has company at the table. Do you like spaghetti?

Babysitter: Yes, thank you.

Prospective Client: Doug goes to bed around eight.

Babysitter: Do you have any pets?

Prospective Client: No pets.

Babysitter: If it's still light out, I can walk over. If it's dark and my parents can't walk me over, will you or your wife be available to pick me up? I don't walk by myself in the dark.

Prospective Client: That's not a problem.

Babysitter: Since I haven't met Doug, I'd like to come half an hour early to get acquainted and learn more about his routines. Would that be okay?

Prospective Client: I'm sure that would be fine. We might even be able to get together a day or two before.

Babysitter: Okay. So I'll talk to my parents and get back to you tomorrow. May I have your phone number and the best time to call?

Prospective Client: Our phone number is 555-5555. The best time to call is between six and nine o'clock in the evening.

Babysitter: Then I'll get back to you between six and nine o'clock tomorrow at 555-5555.

Prospective Client: I'll be looking forward to hearing from you.

Babysitter: Thank you for calling.

Just as special medical needs might influence your decision to accept a job, so might the location. Find out beforehand where the people live, in case it is too far away or in a dangerous neighborhood. The location of a client's house may not seem like a big deal until you find that the drive to and from work eats into your free time. If you decide that you'd like to accept a job that is far from home, discuss your decision with your parents before you take the job. Even though babysitting is your business, your parents have a right to make decisions that affect your safety. By making it a policy to discuss potential jobs with your parents, you can avoid the embarrassment of having to cancel an engagement after you've accepted it.

Discuss transportation details. Don't expect your parents to automatically supply transportation for you. If you have to take a bus to and from the job, ask your clients if they will pay for the fare and the time it takes you to get to and from their house. If you're sitting for a one-parent family that lives far from you, ask that parent who will take you home if the children are asleep. Sometimes the parent will arrange for transportation or give you bus fare if it's still light outside or taxi fare if it's dark.

Things to Consider Before an Interview

Before you interview, consider whether you have any fears that may affect your ability to do a good job. If the family has a pool, and you are afraid of water, you may be better off not babysitting for them. Are you afraid of heights? If the house has more than one story or a circular staircase, it could immobilize you.

Rita learned the first time she sat that she hated babysitting after dark. Once the children went to bed, she felt as though she were in the house alone. She woke one of the youngsters up to keep her company! Afterward, she limited her babysitting to daylight hours.

Are you afraid of, or allergic to, any kind of animal? Howard is allergic to cats, so he won't take a job where there is a cat. He has learned that even if the cat isn't in the house when he's there, he will still have an allergic reaction. Katie is afraid of cats so she always asks about pets during interviews. Then a client who owns a cat knows to put it in the basement or outside where Katie doesn't have to deal with it.

If you have concerns about pets, it's best to ask about them before you babysit. Clients often forget to mention pets during an interview. They think of the animal as just another member of the family. If you're just moderately afraid of dogs, you might be able to establish a relationship with the animal—the same way you do with the children—by visiting ahead of time. If you can't, then request that the animal be put in another room, locked in the basement, or let out in the backyard. If you're still not comfortable, don't babysit for that family.

Michelle would have saved herself some *trauma* if she had asked about pets before taking a job. "It was one of those last-minute jobs, close to home, recommended by a family I trusted," Michelle says. After the parents left, the children told her they had a boa constrictor. "It gave me a creepy feeling to know that thing was in the house. All night I expected it to slither up to me. I was nervous the whole time the kids were up, but I tried not to let them know. If they had known that I was freaked out, they might have let it out.

"After they were in bed, I sat with my feet under me and watched the door to the room the snake was in. I never went back to that house again."

Michelle's sister, Colleen, couldn't wait for the people to call again. When they did, she took the job and asked to hold the snake. Although both teenagers agreed that it wasn't fair of the client not to mention the boa constrictor, their reactions to the pet were different.

Job Responsibilities

One of the most important parts of any interview is clarifying job responsibilities. Ask how many children you will be responsible for, their ages, and exactly what your duties will be. If you're only comfortable caring for two children, and the client has four, it's acceptable to turn down the job. If you can suggest an alternative, such as asking whether someone can help you babysit for a large number of children, don't be afraid to do so. The clients may not be interested, but then again, they may think you are a genius.

Decide if any added job responsibilities, such as doing the dishes, are fair or unreasonable. If the added responsibilities seem like too much work, then tell the clients during the interview that you want to devote your full attention to their children when you babysit. If the clients aren't satisfied with your response, then the interview will be over.

There are always mixed feelings when you don't get a job. But when more is expected of you than you can comfortably deliver, you are better off without that job. Once you start a job and discover that the duties are more than you can handle, it's more difficult to admit. An uncomfortable situation often creates hard feelings. The next chapter describes such a situation.

Chapter Checklist

✓ Preparing for an interview gives you more confidence.

✓ Anticipate potential interview questions and practice your responses.

✓ Think about people who would recommend you, and ask them in advance if you may use them as a reference.

✓ While preparing for an interview, remember to consider your safety.

✓ Determine your policy about babysitting for children who have a contagious illness, require medication on a regular basis, or have special medical needs.

✓ Prepare a substitute babysitter list for clients.

✓ Discuss transportation details.

✓ Be aware of your fears. They may affect your ability to do a good job.

✓ If you are allergic to, or have concerns about, pets, it's best to ask about them before you sit.

✓ Ask how many children you will be responsible for, their ages, and exactly what your duties will be.

✓ Decide if the job responsibilities are fair or unreasonable.

Chapter Six

The Role and Responsibilities of a Babysitter

C armen, a sophomore in high school, got the name and phone number of a potential client from her guidance counselor. When Carmen called to set up the interview, she learned that she'd be watching four-year-old Kevin and two-year-old Dotty during the summer on weekday mornings for about five hours while their father worked and their mother went to school. The father said he'd conduct the interview and that it would take a couple of hours. He wanted to see how Carmen and the children got along. He also requested that Carmen bring references. Carmen agreed that meeting the children was a good idea and assured him that references were not a problem. When Carmen arrived for the interview, the children were playing.

"The father was all business," Carmen remembers. "Not at all what I was used to. But then, I'd never interviewed with a father before. Just mothers. I handed him my references. While he looked at them, I talked to the kids. I was really nervous.

"He asked me if I had any special talents or knew any foreign languages. I said that I did calligraphy, knew a bit of sign language, and was taking Spanish. He said it would be nice if I passed this knowledge on to the children. I thought the kids would enjoy learning sign language, and I was excited about teaching them.

"The father let me know that I'd be expected to get the kids up in the morning, wash, dress, and feed them. He said they were to rest about halfway through the morning, and that if I had time, it would be nice if I vacuumed the floors and folded the clothes in the dryer. But I was never, under any circumstances, to leave either of the children alone. If one child was napping upstairs, I was to stay there and play with the other child until both were awake. He said he was very concerned that his children were well taken care of.

"We discussed salary. I would be paid once a week if I was hired. He said punctuality was a must, and that I was to be there at 6:30 A.M. He said that he and his wife didn't leave until around 7:30, but I needed to be there in case one of the kids woke up. During the interview, I always felt a little off balance, but I thought it was just because the father was so serious.

"Before I left, I read Kevin and Dotty a book. They were like most kids, listening sometimes and jumping off the sofa to play with a toy at other times. I showed them some finger games and got a kick out of watching them try to do them. They weren't a bit shy with me.

"As I left, their father handed me a sheet of paper. When I got home, I realized it was a schedule—practically by the minute—for the kids, and a list of suggested learning activities and experiences."

The job wouldn't start for three weeks, so Carmen concentrated on studying for finals. But when Carmen hadn't heard from the man by the last day of school, she felt unsettled. She definitely wanted a summer job, but she felt she couldn't apply for another one while the first job was on hold. Yet every time Carmen looked at the phone, she saw the man's critical eyes staring at her. Carmen was afraid he'd think she was rushing him. Finally, she called him and said that she needed to know if she had the job or if she should apply elsewhere. The father promised to make a decision before the day ended. That evening, he called to tell Carmen she had the job. He said he'd see her Monday. He emphasized that she be on time.

On Monday, the father greeted Carmen at the door. "He started out by showing me where the dryer was, how to fold the clothes, and where to put them. Then he showed me the kitchen. All the time it was show and tell, show and tell. What the kids could eat, what time they had to eat, and what to do if they didn't eat. We're pretty relaxed at my house, even though Mom doesn't like to see food wasted. But this guy made it sound like a federal offense if you didn't finish what was put in front of you. I was glad I didn't eat there.

"Even after the kids got up, he stood over me and told me what to do and what not to do. He was in total command, and it sounded like he wanted me to be in total command too. A lot of stuff he said was on the paper he'd given me to study at home. But he continued to add stuff that wasn't on the paper. I stopped trying to remember everything he was saying a few minutes after the kids were up. I couldn't keep up with him and the kids too."

Carmen was excited about having a summer job and still having her afternoons free. She figured that once the father was gone, and she was in charge instead of taking orders, everything would be fine.

The first week, everything *was* fine. Carmen arrived early each day, filled with enthusiasm. She set the table for the children's breakfast and decided what they would have. She found that she had time on her hands, so Carmen folded clothes just because they were there, and he'd said, "if you have the time." But Carmen was uncomfortable folding other people's clothes. It was too personal.

She got the vacuuming done by making it a game with the youngsters. But the days were very full, and she was exhausted when she got home. She figured things would improve when she'd worked out a routine. Things are always hard when you start a new job, she reasoned.

One day, Carmen couldn't get the vacuuming done because she couldn't do it when the children were asleep, and there just wasn't any other time. She apologized and explained. The youngsters' father said it was perfectly understandable.

The next week she brought a book to keep her occupied until the children got up, since it bothered her more and more to handle other people's clothing. She decided that she'd fold clothes if she had time, but only the children's clothes and diapers.

After a few weeks, Carmen felt comfortable with the children. She was working her way into a schedule and learning more about the youngsters' likes and dislikes. Also, the children were acting more like themselves with her. At first, they had done or eaten what she'd suggested. Now they were making choices.

One time when Carmen changed Dotty, she put the baby's messy diaper beside the toilet. Before Carmen was finished with Dotty, Kevin ran off. Carmen heard the father's forceful voice in her mind, reminding her not to leave his children alone for an instant. She threw a towel around Dotty and chased after Kevin. Kevin thought it was a great game.

When the father came home, Carmen remembers, "He yelled at me. He was angry that I'd left the diaper [beside the toilet]. I apologized, but he wouldn't listen or give me time to explain. He was angry that I read in the morning instead of folding clothes. He was angry because the vacuuming wasn't always done. He demanded to know what I was doing all day. He accused me of reading instead of paying attention to the kids.

"I started crying, told him he was wrong, and left. I went home and told Mom. She thought maybe I was over-reacting. She wanted me to calm down, call the man, and request time to talk things over reasonably.

"When I agreed, Mom drove me over and sat in the car while I talked inside the house. He rationalized. Before I left, I was convinced that I was wrong and he was right and everything would be okay if I just did what I was supposed to do.

"The next day, Kevin told me I wasn't his mommy or daddy and I couldn't tell him what to do, and if I didn't let him do what he wanted, he was going to have his daddy fire me. I told him to be my guest. I didn't think he could seriously do it, but it bothered me that he felt he could treat me that way."

As the days passed by, Carmen was more and more on edge. Kevin was uncooperative. Carmen went to the child's father for advice. In a demanding tone, in front of Kevin, he said, "You must always be in control!"

Carmen started to put Kevin in a chair for "time-outs." Using the rule of thumb that suggests children can sit in a time-out chair one minute for each year of their age, Carmen limited Kevin to four minutes. However, he misbehaved so often that he was in the chair more than he was out of it, and he would sit unsupervised only for thirty seconds.

Dotty received less attention because of Kevin, and Carmen found it more and more difficult to keep up with picking up after the youngsters—let alone the extra chores. The father criticized Carmen more and more for the cluttered front room. Then, when she picked up toys before leaving, he'd complain that she didn't have the children help her.

One day, Carmen cried all the way home. She was nearly hysterical when she complained to her mom that the man never complimented her—he only criticized. She was angry that he expected her to do things that he'd previously told her to do only "if you have time." And she resented the fact that the children's father criticized her in front of the children. She felt that Kevin's misbehavior was directly related to the way his father spoke to her.

After Carmen calmed down, she decided to talk to the father again. She told him one morning, as he left for work, that she wanted a conference when he got home. Then she called and asked her mother to be waiting in the car if she needed her.

When the children's father returned, Carmen said, "I don't want to be responsible for folding clothes, vacuuming, or any other household chores because it wasn't in the job description. You said 'if I had time.' I don't."

Carmen felt that the man was trying to intimidate her. He glared at her and said, "You are here at 6:30 A.M. The children don't get up until after 7:30. Look at my position. If I pay someone, I have a right to expect them to earn their salary. If you have a job, you have to learn responsibility. If you want to keep your job, you perform your duties. If you don't have anything to do, you find something to do. I'm just, after all, supplying you with busywork."

"I wasn't hired to do household chores," Carmen insisted. "I don't want busywork. I just want to take care of the children. I can come later so you don't have to pay me for that hour." There was a long pause. "All right. Come a half hour later."

Carmen was elated. She hadn't let the man intimidate her, and she'd easily fill that half hour with child-related duties. Now, she assumed, "busywork" was a thing of the past.

The next day, she picked out the youngsters' clothes and set the table. The father told her Kevin was having his tonsils removed that day. Since she only had to watch Dotty, he wanted her to vacuum.

"I thought I made it clear that I didn't want 'busy work,'" Carmen answered. "I am busy enough taking care of the children and keeping up with your written schedule." He replied that Dotty wasn't that difficult to watch.

"That's not the point," Carmen insisted, "I thought we established that I was only hired to babysit. If you want me to do housework, then I expect to be paid extra." His face turned scarlet. "Consider this your last day," he declared and slammed the door.

Instead of being upset, Carmen felt relieved. "I was proud that I'd finally stood up for myself and what I believed." Within half an hour, the father was back and had paid her what he owed her. Carmen didn't know it could feel so good to be fired.

There are no good guys or bad guys in this story. But since the father wanted someone to command, teach, clean house, keep to a strict schedule, and follow his rules, an adult with a military background might have been a better choice than a high school student. Carmen was serious about her role as a babysitter, but her more relaxed attitude reflected the environment she grew up in. It took all her courage to stand up to a person who went from "if you have time" to expecting the job to be done every day. Even a great deal of babysitting had not prepared her for this situation.

As a result of this experience, Carmen now makes it clear to potential clients that she limits her job to babysitting. "If the parents want a tutor, they can hire one. If they want a housekeeper, they can get one. I'm just taking care of the kids," Carmel said. "That doesn't mean I won't teach them something. My mom says I teach them just by being there. Kids are listening all the time. And if I'm only babysitting, it doesn't mean there won't be any cleaning. If the kids eat at the table and leave a mess, I'll wipe the table, clean the chairs they used and, if necessary, sweep the kitchen floor. If we make cookies, we have to clean up after ourselves."

In any work situation, it's important to identify your role and acceptable responsibilities. A babysitter's first responsibility is to the child, but there are other related duties: picking up the toys after a child is finished playing with them (or seeing that the child does it), changing a wet sheet for a dry one before a child takes a nap, helping potty train a child, washing the dishes that were used, and feeding the child a meal.

On the other hand, there are duties that many babysitters would not consider acceptable: stripping beds and remaking them, doing the family laundry, tutoring the child, and washing a week's worth of dishes. Even if you are being paid more money for an extra responsibility, work that distracts your attention from the child may not be acceptable. Watching a child is usually a full-time job, even for adults.

Although you have the right to be respected as a professional, extra responsibility is not necessarily the way a client shows respect. It's easy to confuse responsibility with dependability. Dependability means that you use common sense and can be trusted to do a good job. Responsibility often just means more work. When more work makes you feel as though you've been taken advantage of, it's easy to become resentful. Savvy sitters know that when they're resentful, they're unhappy and they don't do a good job.

Before taking a babysitting job, find out whether your role is strictly child care. Decide what level of responsibility is acceptable to you. If your client crosses your line of acceptability, discuss the problem right away, before it gets out of hand. Most adults will respect your ability to speak up and establish limits. Most parents are aware that people have limitations and their priority is quality care for their children. Clients who need assistance with extra responsibilities may hire you to do those tasks another time. Adults who get upset when a young adult politely stands up for his or her rights probably won't be good clients.

Chapter Checklist

✓ In any work situation, it's important to identify your role and acceptable responsibilities.

✓ Even if you are being paid more money for an extra responsibility, work that distracts your attention from the child may not be acceptable.

✓ Watching a child is usually a full-time job, even for adults.

✓ Savvy sitters know that when they're resentful, they're unhappy and they don't do a good job.

✓ Before taking a babysitting job, clarify whether your role is strictly child care.

✓ Decide what level of responsibility is acceptable to you.

✓ If your client crosses your line of acceptability, discuss the problem right away, before it gets out of hand.

Chapter Seven

Meeting New Families

S uppose you have accepted a babysitting job that's within walking distance of your home. It is your responsibility to meet the two children every day at the bus stop at 3:00 P.M. and walk them home. You are also expected to make an after-school snack for them since neither parent will be home before 6:00.

Within the first few days, the parents don't show up before 6:15—and usually after 6:30. You are getting frustrated. You accepted the babysitting job based on their getting home by 6:00. You counted on them being on time because you are in the school play. Rehearsal is at 7:00, and your mother insists you eat dinner before you go. You tell her that you don't have time to eat, and she says, "If you don't have time for dinner, you'll have to choose between the play and the job."

You should handle this situation by:
a) throwing a tantrum and running to your room
b) calling your customers and telling them you can't babysit
c) quitting the play
d) compromising

Any self-respecting babysitter knows that throwing a tantrum isn't the answer. If you don't do something, your mother will.

The problem with calling and canceling is that it will probably cause you embarrassment and cost you future business. Besides, out of courtesy, it's only fair to give a client time to find a replacement sitter. Most employees give their employers two weeks notice. So, this solution is not an immediate one.

Yes, you could quit the play, but if it means a lot to you, it may be a big sacrifice. You might take your resentment out on others.

Compromising is the best solution. Maybe just presenting the problem to your clients will create a solution. Adults were young once. They know that being in the school play, going to a special dance, or playing a sport is important. If you tell them about the problem—with enough advance notice—often it can be solved. The trick is to bring up conflicts as soon as you are aware of them.

There's an old saying, "A stitch in time saves nine." It means the sooner a problem is uncovered, the easier it is to solve. A problem left unsolved often gets out of hand.

Most parents prefer to know all the facts beforehand to avoid conflict and save time. If possible, discuss any potential conflicts during your interview or "meet the family" visit. If the job is in the evening, and you don't want to babysit past 9:00 P.M. on weekdays because of school, tell your clients. Let them know if you have orthodontist appointments once a month or piano lessons once a week. Your client may need a replacement babysitter on those days. Mention that you can't sit past midnight on Fridays without special permission from your parents, and that you don't babysit on Sunday because that's a family day. If you're a good babysitter, you'll still have plenty of jobs. Parents work around a good babysitter's schedule.

Get-Acquainted Visits

Visiting the children and the household to get acquainted *before* you actually babysit is a good idea. It gives you an opportunity to evaluate the family and your surroundings. It also helps the children to get to know you. Children are more comfortable with someone they have met before.

To make a good impression, wear clothes that say you are ready to play. A piece of simple jewelry is acceptable but leave sharp-edged, child-attracting jewelry at home— babies love to grab dangling earrings. Be sure to smile and pay attention to the children.

Mrs. Nagaishi says, "I look for someone who walks into my house and immediately notices my children. Someone who makes eye contact and talks to them."

This advice is useful for any babysitter. Plan age-appropriate, get-acquainted activities for your first visit with a new family. Babies may not talk, but they love to hear voices, and they see better than many people realize. Infants are partial to bright colors and rhythm. They like singing, even if it's off-key, and rocking.

Children between the ages of one and six may not talk much either, but they are always interested in new things and people. Typically, there's no in-between personality at this age. The child is either very outgoing or very shy—and even outgoing children may be shy around a babysitter. With most children, it's wise not to rush things. Let the child come to you.

If children are old enough to walk, they are old enough to show you where their toys and clothes are. When children know something you don't, it makes them feel important. Children want to be recognized. Ask them about their toys and find out whether they have a favorite. Once you overcome the children's shyness, listen to them. You'll soon learn their interests.

School-age children like tricks and magic. You'll have their attention if you can make a coin appear and disappear, do card tricks, or surprise them with toothpick tricks and puzzles. If you're going to use this tactic to get their attention, keep in mind the age of the child and practice, practice, practice. If the trick you choose takes too long or if it is too complicated, you'll lose a kindergartner's attention. If the trick is not done well or too easy for them to figure out, you'll destroy your credibility. On the other hand, you'll be the hit of the neighborhood if you can fool them and then teach them how to do the trick themselves.

Meeting someone new is like a playing a game of hide-and-seek. Some children's interests are easier to discover than others, and listening to them is often the best way to get acquainted. Once you find the key to their individuality, you'll be one step closer to winning the game.

It's hard to guess children's interests because each child is so different. A fifth grader name Phillip hates to read. Heidi, one of Phillip's classmates, is in the process of teaching herself Chinese. A game of basketball will put you on Phillip's good side, especially if you can give him some hints on how to beat his dad. On the other hand, Heidi will be proud to show you how Chinese characters often resemble what they represent.

Meeting the Parents

The relationship between you and the children you babysit is usually more intimate than the one you develop with their parents. But both relationships are equally important. Sometimes your relationship with the parents determines whether or not you will continue to work for them.

Visiting the family might save you from a bad employment situation. Gretta recommends, "If you get a creepy feeling about the parents, don't babysit for them. Even though you don't have to be around them much, they can make things pretty uncomfortable. Just say you're busy."

Joey says, "If I don't like the kids' parents, I just tell them my mom and dad said no. Then I tell my parents what's going on so they can back me up."

Katie feels safer and more self-assured when her mom or dad come along for the first visit. She suggests, "If you don't know the people, check out the house first. And, take at least one of your parents with you." If something doesn't seem right, her parents give her an easy exit.

Sometimes a problem with a parent doesn't become obvious until you've been babysitting for a while. The issue may be something as simple as a personality conflict or as complicated as drug abuse. If you feel uncomfortable with the parent or the home environment, trust your feelings. Don't take the job! Turning down a job at any time is acceptable. If you're concerned that your friends may be asked to sit for a certain family and be put in a bad situation, simply tell your friends that you won't babysit for that family. However, before you tell anyone that a family is off-limits for you, talk it over with a trusted adult to see whether they agree that sharing this usually confidential information is appropriate.

Chapter Checklist

✓ Discuss any potential conflicts during your interview or first visit.

✓ Visiting the children and the household to get acquainted *before* you actually babysit is a good idea.

✓ Children are more comfortable with someone they have met before.

✓ To make a good impression, wear clothes that say you are ready to play, smile, and pay attention to the children.

✓ Plan age-appropriate, get-acquainted activities for your first visit to a new family.

✓ With most children, it's best not to rush things. Let the child come to you.

✓ Listen to the children and discover their interests.

✓ The relationship between you and the children you babysit is usually more intimate than the one you develop with their parents. But both relationships are equally important. If you feel uncomfortable with the parents or the home environment, trust your feelings. Don't take the job!

Chapter Eight

Professionals Ask

Every other Saturday for the past three months, the routine has been the same. Dennis babysits eight-year-old Fred and ten-year-old Tina for their mother, Ms. Hedges, from 10:30 A.M. to 1:30 P.M. Ms. Hedges arranged for Dennis to order pizza to be delivered for his and the children's lunch.

The children's father, Mr. Wall, has an apartment across town and picks the children up on occasional weekends. Dennis has never met Mr. Wall.

One Saturday morning, Dennis orders a Hawaiian pizza at 11:30. He sets the table and pours drinks. About fifteen minutes later, the doorbell rings. Dennis opens the door with money in his hand for the delivery person, but the man at the door says, "Hi. I'm Fred and Tina's dad. Are they ready to go?"

What should Dennis do?

a) Slam and lock the door in the man's face.

b) Let the children go.

c) Say, "Excuse me a minute. I wasn't expecting you," then close and lock the door and call Ms. Hedges.

d) Ask the children if they have plans with their father.

e) Let the man in, then call Ms. Hedges.

You probably know that the best answer is *c*. But, if Dennis was concerned or felt threatened, it would be okay for him to slam the door and lock it in the man's face. It's always better to be safe than sorry. Letting the children go with their father or asking them if they have plans with him aren't good answers. Dennis has to answer to the children's mother because she hired him, and the children might say they have plans with their father just because going out with their dad sounds like more fun than staying home with a sitter. It's possible that Ms. Hedges might have forgotten to tell Dennis about the planned outing for the children, but he can't take that chance.

Never let a parent in if you don't know him or her or haven't been instructed to do so by the parent who hired you—even if the children vouch for that parent. The parent may be a great person or may be a troublemaker. Remember that it isn't your fault if a parent forces their way in and takes their children. Just try to stay calm and get any information you can, such as the color and make of their vehicle, a license plate number, a description of the person and their clothes, or what the children were wearing. Then, call the police *first,* and the parent who hired you *second.*

There's an old saying: "The only dumb question is the one you don't ask." Professionals always ask.

Babies, Toddlers, and Preschoolers

The younger the child, the more important it is to ask the parent where to find diapers, changing equipment, extra clothes, and bedding. Babies can't tell you if they have a pacifier or a favorite blanket—or if that missing blanket is why you're having trouble putting them to sleep. They can't tell you whether they get an iced teething ring. They can't show you where their coat and hat are kept.

Parents sometimes forget to tell babysitters where coats are kept or what the child's routine is. Parents live and deal with these details every day, and they don't see them as out of the ordinary. Spencer has *colic.* Every night, between 8:00 P.M. and 10:00 P.M., the only thing that comforts him is to be walked. Not rocked, *walked.* Bonnie sleeps for half an hour after each feeding and is very active for the next three hours or so—even at night. If you go to either house with a pile of homework, expecting to do it while the baby sleeps, it's likely you'll end up doing homework into the wee hours at home. So don't be afraid to ask in advance if there are any special situations or preferences. Knowing how to handle them will pay off. You're not a mind reader.

Toddlers and *preschoolers* often have imaginary friends, so ask clients about them. If the child has an imaginary friend, ask its name and how seriously you are supposed to take this friend. You might ask if it is okay to admit that you don't see the imaginary friend.

More important, ask about house rules. Even with babies, there are house rules. Check to see if it is okay to take the baby for a walk during daylight hours. If it's acceptable to leave the house, make sure you know where the extra key is hidden or if a neighbor has a key. If the neighbor isn't home, is it okay for you to take the baby to your house? If not, what is acceptable? Some parents, especially new ones, want absolute quiet when the baby is napping. Ask if it is okay to play the radio or watch TV when the baby is asleep. If not, don't bring your Walkman. The earphones could block out an infant's cry.

When you're babysitting for toddlers and preschoolers, there are other things to consider. Ask whether the child takes naps at a set time. If so, ask about the routine, such as whether the bedroom door should be open or closed. If the parent is in the midst of potty training, you need to know whether the child wears diapers or training pants and whether there is a set schedule or a particular technique that works best.

Barry was eighteen months old and just beginning potty training when his teenage cousins came to sit. They wanted to put Barry down for a nap, but he was supposed to go to the bathroom before he went to bed. They held him over the toilet, but he demanded a drink of water. They offered him one while they held the glass, but he insisted on holding the glass while he was held over the toilet. They gave him the glass. He poured the water on his stomach, went to the bathroom, and said, "There," with a sigh of satisfaction.

When Barry's mom came home, she told her nieces that she believed little boys were easier to train if you dribbled a little water down their front. But Barry's mom had failed to let her nieces in on her strategy.

School-Age Children

School-age children bring their own challenges to babysitters. The older the child, the more important it is to talk to parents about established house rules. Some children have a built-in urge to test the sitter's knowledge of house rules. Researching them could mean the difference between calm and conflict. Rules about television viewing, bedtimes, and snacks vary from one family to another.

There are also a number of questions to ask concerning homework. Is there a special time when or where they are to do homework? Are you allowed to help? Do the youngsters use a computer for homework? Are they allowed to go online? Are any online sites off-limits? Is there a time restriction? After their homework is done, can the children play computer games? Are any of these games considered inappropriate?

Many families set limits on video games, so it's a good idea to ask about them too. Morgan's video-game limit is fifteen minutes a night. Rules about the time limit and type of game he can play are strictly enforced and depend on his behavior. If he doesn't behave and cooperate, he doesn't get to play video games. Sometimes an older child is allowed to play certain video games only when the younger one is asleep.

Phone limitations are common too. If children are allowed to talk on the phone, ask about a time limit. In some families, children are allowed to answer the phone. In others, only the adult or the babysitter may answer the phone. If you're uncomfortable with a child answering the phone, say so. Many families have call waiting and caller ID services. It is not always easy to figure out how to use these features on different brands of telephones. If you're supposed to answer the phone, ask the parent to demonstrate how to use it.

Sometimes various areas of the house are off-limits. The basement may be out of bounds because it contains exercise equipment or tools that the children cannot use without adult supervision. The living room may be out of bounds to anyone with food or drink. Parents often declare their bedroom off-limits.

Other families are strict about plans being finalized by the parents. School-age children often want to have a friend over. Some parents will allow the sitter to decide whether their child can go to another house to play or whether a friend can come over. Even in this situation, there are limits. Make sure you have the facts—names, phone numbers, description. Do not, under any circumstances, let a child leave with anyone if the parents didn't tell you that the outing was arranged for and approved. It is better to have an angry grandmother than a missing child.

Television and Videos

You can't be expected to know another family's house rules unless they are written down or you have been their regular sitter for a long time. Anything parents feel strongly about, they'll usually mention. For instance, the parents of one preschooler have an extensive library of videos that they feel are appropriate for their daughter. But the mother says, "I'm not paying a teenager to have a video do the babysitting. I prefer that there's a balance and that there is some creative responsibility on the part of the sitter." The mother adds, "I feel very strongly about my daughter not watching commercial TV."

Some parents of preschool children are more lenient, and they allow their youngsters to watch children's shows on television. At the same time, the parents count on their babysitter to use good judgment when it comes to which shows the little ones should watch. If the parents you're sitting for don't have strict TV, movie, and video rules, consider the age of the child. Young children are easily frightened. If you like to watch horror shows, watch them at home. Although you may use what you are allowed to do at your home as a general guide, remember that rules change from family to family. Never assume. Always ask.

Electronic Equipment

A couple had arranged for their favorite babysitter to watch their sons while they attended a business dinner, but the sitter became ill on the day of the dinner. The father's boss recommended a high school student as a replacement babysitter. The girl showed up at the last minute, so the mother showed her where the boys' beds and necessities were, gave her the phone number where they could be reached, and dashed out the door. When the couple returned later that evening, the babysitter was sprawled on the floor surrounded by compact discs.

Although the couple hadn't told the sitter that the CD player was off-limits, they felt their privacy had been invaded. The mother complained, "I know the discs are supposed to have a long life, but only if they are well taken care of. My discs were on the rug, picking up lint, which affects the player. I had them filed on the very top shelf of my bookcase. The babysitter had to get a stepstool to reach them. I was so upset I had to leave the room and let my husband deal with her. She'll never babysit at my house again."

Not only will that babysitter never work for that family again, she probably won't ever find out why she isn't asked back. Mistakes like these keep a babysitting business from expanding, but you can't correct a problem if you don't know it exists. In this case, the parents didn't have time to tell the babysitter not to use the CD player.

Do your parents have any electronic equipment that no one else is allowed to use? Is there some equipment that you can use if you ask permission? If you're familiar with such limits, use them as a guide for yourself and your charges. If you do not know whether you or the children are allowed to use certain equipment, the safest decision is not to use it. Then write yourself a reminder note to ask for guidelines the next time. Even if you find out that using the equipment is acceptable, parents appreciate it when you discuss it with them first.

Discipline

Ask parents in advance about their method of discipline. Joseph said, "I like for the parents to say it in front of the kids. That way they know that I know what to do and have permission to do it. Then they are more cooperative." Find out how to handle arguments between siblings. Although a good rule of thumb is not to take sides, parents often have specific hints they can share with you.

Lidia wishes she had been more informed before she sat for a little neighborhood girl she'd played with a few times. She says, "The first time I sat with her, I had to call home to ask my own parents what to do when she refused to go to bed. She wasn't very interested in obeying me when she didn't want to."

Lidia believes she and the child were too close in age and the little girl saw her as a playmate rather than someone with authority. "That was the beginning and ending of my babysitting career," she says. But if Lidia had asked the little girl's parents what to do if the child didn't cooperate, her career might have lasted longer.

Even if a child has seriously crossed the line of acceptable behavior, never strike a child in your care. Annette says, "Even if the parents give me permission, I don't hit the kids. I feel that hitting them teaches them to hurt others."

If parents don't give any suggestions regarding discipline, most babysitters agree that time-outs work best for children who misbehave. Depending on the age of the child, sitting in a chair in the same room you are in, or going to their own room, works best. Henry says, "I have them sit on the chair. After about a minute, I talk to them about what they did. Then I give them a hug so they know I'm not going to stay mad at them."

It's just as important—if not more important—to recognize what children do right. "Look at that. You picked up all the puzzle pieces and put them in the box. Now they will all be there the next time you want to play with the puzzle," or "You know how to put on your coat." If you look for the best in youngsters, you'll usually get it.

Sitting at Night

If you expect to be sitting at night, ask about the children's sleeping habits. Find out whether older children are allowed to read themselves to sleep. Even school-age children might be afraid of the dark or need a night-light. Sometimes a hall light has to be left on until the children are asleep.

Many children follow a ritual that makes them more comfortable about going to bed. Some children need to put on their pajamas, have a cookie, brush their teeth, and have two or three books read to them—in that order. If things are done out of order, they can't fall asleep.

Suppose a parent tells you that a child is in the habit of going right to sleep and sleeping through the night, but the child won't go to sleep for you. Forcing the issue seldom works. Some children are uncomfortable when their parents leave. Ask them if they want to be held or if they would like for you to lie down with them. If the answer is no, respect their wishes. If they confess to being afraid of ghosts, don't laugh. Ask them if their parents have a secret way of getting rid of ghosts, or tell them about your own fear of ghosts and how you resolved it.

When Daniel told Julia he was afraid of ghosts, she asked the ghost's name. "It doesn't have one," he said. So Julia told Daniel about her family's pet ghost—Judy. "The best thing about Judy," Julia said, "was that we could blame everything on her. If there was water on the bathroom floor, and no one wanted to admit they did it, we blamed Judy." Daniel decided to name his ghost Grover. Once Grover had a name, he wasn't so frightening anymore.

Chapter Checklist

✓ Never let a parent in if you have not been instructed to do so by the parent who hired you—even if the children vouch for that parent.

✓ Babies can't tell anyone where to find the things needed for their care. Ask the parent where to find a baby's clothing, supplies, and equipment.

✓ Ask about potty training, imaginary friends, and bedtime routines.

✓ Ask about house rules—even for babies.

✓ The older the child, the more important it is to talk to parents about established house rules. Television viewing, bedtime, and snacks can vary from one family to another.

✓ Never assume. Always ask.

✓ If you do not know whether you or the children are allowed to use certain equipment, the safest decision is not to use it.

✓ Establish limits for yourself: food, snacks, electronic equipment, and phone.

✓ If parents don't give any suggestions regarding discipline, most babysitters agree that time-outs work best for children who misbehave.

✓ If you expect to be sitting at night, inquire about the children's sleeping habits.

Chapter Nine

Meals and Snacks

Matt meets six-year-old Jimmy and eight-year-old Stephanie at their school every day and walks them home. The youngsters are allowed to have the healthy snack that their mother, Ms. Breken, prepared for them and Matt. Matt appreciates the fact that he is included, especially since he's hungry after school, but he has never enjoyed Ms. Breken's healthy snacks.

What should Matt do?

a) Bring something to eat while the youngsters are eating what their mother prepared.

b) Go without a snack.

c) Treat the youngsters to an ice cream cone.

d) Bring along the ingredients for cookies, and substitute them for the prepared snack.

e) Ask the children's mother if there is something else he can eat or bring to eat.

Children like to imitate the babysitter, especially if they admire him or her. Matt needs to keep this in mind before he makes his decision. Going without the snack, substituting a different one—such as an ice cream cone—or eating a different one can cause problems. Disregarding a parent's instructions is asking for trouble. Health conditions, such as diabetes, could dictate that Jimmy must eat a certain food at a specific time, or Stephanie may want to try Matt's snack even though she's allergic to it.

The best thing Matt can do is to talk about the snack situation with Ms. Breken and ask her if there is something else he can eat or bring to eat. She probably has a good reason for choosing the snacks that she does, and it might not have occurred to her that Matt doesn't like them. If Matt and her children have a good relationship, Ms. Breken might work out a snack plan that pleases everyone.

Food Allergies

Parents with children who do not tolerate sugar well or have a food allergy make sure the food in their house is safe for their children to eat. In fact, if you regularly sit for children who have allergies, you may think you already know what foods are off limits. *Don't you believe it.* Parents who have children with food allergies check every ingredient and additive listed on food labels. Parents become experts at spotting questionable ingredients when their child's health depends on it.

Children who are allergic to milk products cannot eat ice cream, cheese, or many packaged foods. Children who are allergic to peanuts can become seriously ill from eating anything cooked in, or prepared with, peanut oil. Youngsters may not realize how serious their allergy is, so don't ever eat anything in front of these children that they cannot tolerate. They may be tempted to sneak a little taste and then have a severe reaction. Food allergies are dangerous. Although most parents will mention a child's food allergies to the sitter, it's best to ask about them.

Even if the children have no known allergies, discuss any food that you want to bring to a babysitting job with the children's parents. Children may not be allowed to eat certain foods due to their religious beliefs, or their food choices may be limited because the family is vegetarian. If parents approve snacks that you bring, don't ever eat anything in front of children that you are not willing to share.

Infants and Babies

By the time you are old enough to babysit, milk has become just something to drink. But for babies, it is a nutritious meal. Even after solid food is introduced, milk may still be the baby's primary food.

Infants may drink breast milk or formula. Formula can be made from cow's milk, goat's milk, or soy products. Milk from a human mother meets all the nutritional needs of the human baby and is easier for the child to digest. Cow's milk is perfect for calves but must be modified into formula for human babies. Formula from goat's milk or soy milk is most often used when a baby is allergic to cow's milk. Be sure to ask what kind of milk the baby gets. Always wash your hands with soap and water before preparing a baby's bottle.

A mother who nurses her baby pumps breast milk into a container for storage so that others can feed the baby when she is away. When a babysitter is expected, the milk is usually stored in the refrigerator in a bottle. The mother probably keeps an extra supply of her milk in a container in the freezer for unexpected circumstances.

Do not use hot water to thaw or heat breast milk. Heat destroys the milk's *immune* properties. Mother's milk carries *antibodies* that pass through the mother's body to her baby during breast-feeding. This process is nature's way of protecting a baby until the immune system is fully developed.

A nursing infant is used to having warm milk. To warm breast milk that has been stored in the refrigerator, place the bottle in a measuring cup or bowl of warm water and wait for about five minutes. Check the temperature of the milk by sprinkling it onto the inside of your wrist. Don't try to test for warmth with your fingers. They are covered with a thicker layer of skin and are less sensitive than your wrist. If the milk is not warm enough, replace the warm water and wait again.

Frozen breast milk takes about half an hour to thaw. Unless you enjoy holding a screaming, hungry baby, figure out when the baby will be hungry, and thaw the bottle ahead of time. To thaw breast milk, hold the container under warm, running water, or place the container in a bowl of warm water for about half an hour. Do not microwave breast milk. Microwaves often heat foods unevenly and can alter the composition of the milk.

Formula comes in both liquid and powdered form. Some liquid forms need to be diluted with water, and others do not. Make sure you know the difference between the two types of formula. If you have to open the formula, wash your hands, the top of the formula container, and the can opener with soap and water and rinse well. Shake the can of liquid formula before opening.

Use a plastic scoop to measure powdered formula. Although there are directions on formula containers, it is always best to ask parents for directions on how to prepare the baby's bottle. Too much formula mixture in a bottle is harmful to the baby.

Ask the parents what kind of water to use to dilute the formula. Bottled water may be available. If you use water from the faucet, use cold water because sediments collect in hot-water tanks. Also, hot water dissolves lead, copper, and metals more easily than cold water. Because babies are small, they are very susceptible to metal poisoning. For infants, you may need to boil the water and let it cool before mixing it with the formula.

If the bottle is already prepared, find out whether the baby drinks milk warm or cold. If the child prefers warm milk, never heat a bottle in the microwave. Although the outside of the bottle may feel cool, the milk inside may be hot, and a child's mouth and throat could be burned. Instead, run hot water into a measuring cup or bowl and let the bottle stand in the water for about five minutes. Hot water does not change the composition of formula. Always shake the bottle, then test the milk's warmth. If the temperature is not correct, repeat the process described above to warm the bottle, or run cold water over the bottle to cool it. Always retest the milk.

Besides making sure that the milk is prepared properly and heated to the right temperature, there are other safety concerns when feeding babies. Milk may become contaminated if you reuse plastic bottle liners or save bottles from one feeding to the next. And don't ever support a baby's bottle by placing something under or against it instead of holding it. A baby can choke easily. Even if babies are old enough to hold their own bottle, don't leave them alone to drink it. You should cradle the child in your arms or on your lap.

Once the baby begins drinking, it's important to be sure that the baby doesn't suck air instead of milk. Even when you're careful to hold the bottle at the right angle, a baby still swallows some air. Burping gets rid of any swallowed air.

To burp a baby, protect your clothes with a cloth diaper or receiving blanket, then drape the baby over your shoulder or your knees, and pat or rub the baby's back firmly but gently. If the air bubble does not escape within two or three minutes, change the baby's position and try again. Babies often spit up small amounts when they burp. But, if the amount of spit up seems like a lot to you, or comes out with great force, tell the parents when they get home.

Sometimes parents show the babysitter how their baby likes to be held while drinking a bottle and burping. Each baby has his or her own personality, likes, and dislikes, and parents know their baby best. If the parents don't demonstrate or describe their baby's preferences, ask about them.

Meals are important for babies, so try to make feeding time a pleasant experience for them. When sitting for babies who are ready for solid food, try to stay calm even when the bowl of cereal ends up on the floor or on the baby's head. Babies like to play with their food. Remember that you have the advantage since the baby is in an infant seat or a high chair. This strategy keeps the mess in one spot. Before you begin feeding the baby, make sure that you strap the child in the seat or chair snugly and know how the high-chair tray locks and releases. Then put a bib on the baby, and keep your sense of humor handy—along with a warm washcloth. Never leave a baby unattended in a high chair. Let the phone ring and the doorbell go unanswered.

Many parents and babysitters have feeding strategies. If you give the baby one spoon while you use another, it helps distract him from grabbing the feeding spoon. Or, if you have the parents' permission, you might give the baby finger food to investigate between bites. If a child turns his or her head away, he or she is finished eating. Don't try to force a child to eat—doing so frustrates both of you. Parents often have clues that will help you get more food into the baby than on the high chair or the floor. Again, it's helpful to ask for hints ahead of time.

Toddlers

Feeding a baby often takes all your attention, so feeding yourself at the same time is usually a lost cause. But when a baby becomes a toddler, he or she needs your company and example while eating. Toddlers want to do everything that you do. When you wash your hands before you prepare their food and before you eat, they will want to wash their hands too. If you sit at the table when you have a meal, they will want to eat there too. If you screw your face up at vegetables, guess who won't eat vegetables for mom and dad later?

Toddlers believe they can do anything. They want to pull the milk out of the refrigerator and pour it. They want to get the bread off the counter, the jam out of the cupboard, the knife out of the drawer, and make their own sandwich. If you can think of a snack that the toddler can prepare on his or her own, you will be a big hero. But make sure "on his or her own" doesn't happen when your back is turned.

Children this age are very busy, prefer to eat with their hands, and find it difficult to sit still long enough to eat. However, children who play while eating can choke. Not only can careless behavior contribute to choking, so can certain foods. Many parents don't want their children to eat grapes, hot dogs, candy, or popcorn because they can choke easily on these four foods. Avoid them when possible, but if parents approve them, use caution when serving them, and be sure to cut them in small pieces. Always ask parents what foods, drinks, and snacks to give their children, how much to give them, and if there are any special food-related instructions.

Mr. Lee likes to have half of a jelly sandwich, cut in half, prepared for his daughter, Tina, at lunchtime. He wants part of the sandwich offered with half a cup of milk in a sipper cup. If Tina is still hungry, she can have the rest of the sandwich. If Tina doesn't eat lunch, she doesn't get an afternoon snack.

Ms. Tish gives Billy a choice. He may have soup or a toasted-cheese sandwich. If Billy doesn't eat his lunch, he can have an apple for a snack later. If he does eat lunch, he gets cookies for a snack.

Every family is different, so it's important to inquire about meals and snacks. Do the children eat at a particular time? If you have a tea party, can the children drink real tea? Is it all right to have a picnic? Do the children have special place mats, dishes, and silverware? Are the children expected to use table manners?

Preschoolers and School-Age Children

Many of the questions a babysitter might ask about meals and snacks for toddlers also apply to preschoolers and school-age children. Here are some meal-related questions to consider when sitting for older children: Are there any rules about meals? Are there any rules about snacks? How do the parents feel about the children eating in front of the television or sitting at the table? Do the children set the table and clear away the dishes afterward? Are they permitted to cut their own food with knives? Does the family say grace?

Is there any food in the cupboard or refrigerator that is off-limits to you or the children? Just because there is food and that looks like leftovers doesn't mean that the parents want you or the children to eat it. The leftover soup may be the father's lunch for tomorrow. The big stack of chips and cases of pop may be for Friday night's party. Well-organized parents often prepare meals in advance. So find out what is appropriate to eat.

Preschoolers and school-age children usually know what they want to eat, when they want it, and how they want it. Find out if they are allowed to prepare their own food, and if so, whether they can use the micro-wave oven or the stove. If you feel uncomfortable about sitting children who prepare their own food, be sure to speak up.

Chapter Checklist

✓ Food allergies are dangerous. Although most parents will mention a child's food allergies to the sitter, it's best to ask about them.

✓ Discuss any food that you want to bring to a babysitting job with the children's parents.

✓ Be sure to ask what kind of milk the baby gets. Know where to find and how to prepare the bottle.

✓ Always wash your hands before preparing a baby bottle.

✓ Check the temperature of the milk by sprinkling it onto the inside of your wrist. Don't try to test for warmth with your fingers.

✓ Don't ever support a baby's bottle by placing something under or against it instead of holding it.

✓ Ask parents for hints on feeding and burping positions that work best for their infant.

✓ Never leave a baby unattended in a high chair.

✓ Ask parents about the best strategy for feeding solid foods to their baby or toddler.

✓ Careless behavior can contribute to choking, and so can certain foods, such as grapes, hot dogs, candy, and popcorn.

✓ Always ask parents what foods, drinks, and snacks to give their children, how much to give them, and if there are any special food-related instructions.

✓ Ask whether any food or beverages are off-limits to you or the children.

Chapter Ten

Safety

Maggie was hired to sit for two-year-old twins Trisha and Troy while their parents go shopping. Before the parents leave, the twins' mom helps Maggie put the youngsters' coats on and leads everyone to the fenced backyard. She shows Maggie where the twins' pedal cars are stored, says good-bye to her children, and goes into the house. Maggie hears the parents' car pull out of the driveway as she plays traffic cop for the children.

About half an hour later, the children want to go inside. Maggie helps them out of their cars, and they tramp to the back door. Troy tries to open the door. Maggie isn't concerned when it doesn't open. Troy is little, she thinks, and he isn't strong enough to open the door. But when Maggie tries it, she discovers that the door is locked.

Not a problem, Maggie thinks. She unlocks the back gate, holds the children's hands, and they head for the front door. It's also locked.

What should Maggie do?

a) Take the children to a neighbor's house to see if they have a key.

b) Break a window so she can get in.

c) Call the twins' parents from the neighbor's house or the nearby store.

d) Check the house to see if there is any other way to get in.

e) Call her parents.

Maggie's common sense and quick thinking saved the day. She noticed that the bathroom window was open, and the opening was large enough for her to fit through. So she told the children that they had an important job. To help her open the door, they had to sit in their pedal cars and honk the horns loudly. Their honking, she told them, would magically get her into the house. When she was sure that the twins were convinced of their big role, she put them in their cars, locked the gate, and reminded them to honk until she appeared again. Then she ran to the window, pulled herself up and over the sill, dashed through the house, swung open the back door, and shouted, "You did it!" By involving the children in the solution to her problem, Maggie was able to distract their attention away from what she was doing. She had them safely corralled in the backyard, and she was able to hear them.

Going to the neighbors would have been a good plan, but Maggie hadn't met any of the neighbors yet, and she didn't see anyone around. All the information about where to reach the parents was posted by the phone inside the house, so she couldn't call the twins' parents.

Maggie says she would have, somehow, called her own parents if she hadn't found a way into the house. But not in a million years would she have broken a window to get into the house. Not only would she have destroyed property, she might have cut herself, and the broken window would give others access to the house. Perhaps you can think of other safe ways that Maggie could have handled this situation.

Nobody knows how he or she will respond in an emergency until it happens. Most people respond more calmly if they have considered emergency situations, and their possible responses, beforehand. Sometimes preparing your response means asking your clients safety-related questions in advance or arming yourself with information. Role-playing safety situations with babysitting friends or your parents is good practice and can make the difference between panicking and handling a situation calmly.

Planning Ahead

One of the best things you can do as a sitter is to prepare two emergency cards—one beside the phone and one in your pocket. This advice may sound silly, but even adults can forget their address and phone number in an emergency. How likely is it that you'll remember the address where you're babysitting? List the address (include the cross streets), the telephone number with the area code, and the name of your client on your information cards. Other handy information includes where to reach the children's parents (including cellular phone numbers and pager numbers); who to call if you can't reach the parents; and phone numbers for the poison center; the police, the fire department; and the children's doctor. If you are too nervous to dial a phone number, dial 0 to get an operator who is trained to help.

Many parents have beepers and can be paged in an emergency. If you've never called a beeper before, ask your client to demonstrate how the system works. Neil says that most of his clients have beepers, so he developed a code for various situations. If he has a question that he feels needs an answer before the parents come home, he calls the beeper and leaves the family's home phone number. If one of the children suddenly becomes ill, or the toilet overflows, Neil follows the home number with 311, signaling that the call is important. If Neil has to call for emergency help, he adds 911 to the home number.

Know the Layout

Statistics show that 95 percent of child-related accidents can be prevented. So, think about safety and prevention. Parents are counting on you to spot potential danger so that it can be averted. Ask your clients to walk you through their house, showing you its safety features and describing their safety procedures. Check to see if there is a pool. If there is, ask about the rules concerning it. Ask where the smoke alarms are located and whether the family has any established fire-escape routes or instructions. Ask whether the family members have a designated meeting place in case of fire or another emergency. If you're babysitting in a two-story house, check to see whether there is a fire ladder or a balcony with outside stairs.

You should also ask if: there is a fire extinguisher and how it works, where the furnace/air-conditioning thermostat is located, whether you can change the setting, where the shut-off valves are for the gas and water, where the circuit-breaker box and a flashlight are located, whether there is a burglar-alarm system and how it works.

Keep your eyes open for light switches. Does the house have timers that automatically turn lights off or on? There's nothing more startling than being in a new place and having a light or radio come on unexpectedly.

A ringing telephone can be a distraction. Make sure you know the location of the telephone, emergency information, and paper and pencils to take telephone messages. Does the household have caller ID or a telephone-answering machine? If so, consider requesting that the answering device be turned on while you're sitting. That way, you can screen calls when the phone rings, and you won't get distracted. Be sure you know how to stop the machine and take the call if it sounds important.

If there is no answering machine or the client prefers that you answer the phone, practice phone safety. Let the caller know that Mr. and Mrs. Customer are busy, but you will be glad to take a message and have them return the call when they're free. If the caller asks whether you know when Mr. or Mrs. Customer will return the call, answer

100

"No. They told me not to disturb them. But I'll give them the message as soon as I can." If the call is urgent, most callers will leave a message, and you can relay it. For your own safety, never tell the caller that you are a babysitter or what time you expect the children's parents. Never give out any information about the household. Don't even repeat the phone number where you are. If a caller thinks he or she has dialed the wrong number, ask what number the caller was trying to reach.

Just as you may have to answer the phone, you may have to answer the door. Ask your clients for guidelines. Are there any rules about answering the door? For instance, is there a relative who may drop by unexpectedly? Who can be allowed entrance? Ask for a description of anyone who can come in. If someone other than the parent is going to relieve you, how will it be handled? If people aren't expected, is it okay to pretend there is nobody at home? Is there a peephole in the door? Unless you have specific instructions to do otherwise, do not open the door to anyone you don't know.

Keep doors, including sliding glass doors, and windows locked at all times. Unlocked doors and windows, day or night, are an invitation to unwanted visitors. Know how the door locks work and test them. One sitter was locked out of the house with her two charges because she didn't know that she had to pull the door toward her for the key to turn the lock.

Outside lights are a wonderful deterrent to intruders at night. But lights inside a house with the drapes open are a different story. Even a small lamp illuminates a room like stage lights in a theater. If it's dark enough to turn on an inside light, be sure to close the drapes.

Safety for Babies

The good thing about new babies is that, if you use common sense, it's relatively easy to keep them safe. But even small infants can throw themselves out of your arms, so always hold them with both hands.

Babies put everything in their mouths, so choking is a safety issue. Prevent this hazard by removing any objects that are smaller than the child's fist before putting a baby down.

Crawling babies are explorers and investigators. Since they don't know the danger around them, they need supervision every single minute they're awake. Crawl or lie on the floor, and scan the play area for electrical cords, wobbly furniture, and anything that can be pulled over on the child. One four-month-old grabbed a stool, and it fell on him, breaking his collarbone.

If unsafe items can't be moved, block out a safe area. Never leave a crawling baby alone, even if the baby falls asleep on the floor. When the baby wakes, her natural curiosity will lead to mischief. So if you don't want to disturb the child, find a book to read, do homework, or write in your diary—but stay with the baby.

If the phone rings while you are diapering a baby, let it ring. Do not leave the baby alone, even for a second. Never leave a baby on a diapering table even if he or she is belted in. Healthy babies can kick their way into unsafe positions. Don't leave a newborn unattended on a sofa or bed either.

Some babies are born with the crawling instinct and never lose it. The only safe places to leave babies are in cribs or playpens.

Before putting the baby to bed, check the *bassinet* or crib for unsafe items in or around it. Drapery and mini-blind cords need to be tied out of the baby's reach. When you put the baby down for a nap, clear the bed of toys and pillows. Also, it's not safe to put babies to bed facedown. Ask the parents in advance about their baby's sleeping position. Most babies sleep on their backs or sides.

Safety for Toddlers

Toddlers are so curious about the world around them that they are probably the most difficult children to keep safe. They are also copycats, so keep that in mind at all times. If they see you eating, they want to eat. If you take an aspirin, they want one too. If you comb your hair, they follow suit. They want to investigate everything.

One father discovered his two-year-old daughter sitting in the top drawer of a bureau, with lipstick from ear to ear, powder from head to toe, and several bottles of make-up surrounding her. She had tugged the drawers out and used them as a ladder.

Just because cleaning supplies are on a high shelf doesn't mean that a toddler won't find a way to get to them. Toddlers are ingenious at figuring out how to get to the highest place in the house or how to hide in the smallest. Never leave toddlers alone for an instant. If you're in the kitchen making lunch, strap a toddler into the high chair. Give him or her a spoon, a plastic cup, or some other toy to play with. Although a high chair can keep a child out of harm's way, it is not meant for restraint. If you leave the room, take the child with you.

Even if the child is safely belted in a high chair, practice good kitchen safety habits. Never leave knives or other sharp items close to the edge of the counter, and after use, keep utensils in a safe place. All appliance cords need to be coiled behind the appliance so that they can't be pulled. Use the back burners of the stove when you heat food, and turn pot handles toward the back of the stove. If you have something warming on the stove, make sure the little explorer is with you when you leave the room. Everything is tempting to toddlers.

Don't underestimate toddlers just because they can't talk. Watch their actions and the twinkle in their eye. Children of this age still put things in their mouths—one more reason for not turning your back on them. First-aid training is especially helpful in case a child chokes. The *Heimlich maneuver* used for infants and small children is not the same as the one for older children and adults.

Poisoning is another big concern at this age. Most parents childproof bathrooms because they are safety hazards, but if the medicine cabinet is not childproof, close the bathroom door. Does the toilet have a child-safety lock on it? How does it work? Does the bathroom door have a lock on it? Can children get locked in? Is there a way into the bathroom even when the door is locked from the inside?

Electrical shocks are also a potential hazard. Make sure the child does not go near electrical outlets. Many parents plug up outlets, but keep children away from them anyway.

Little adventurers like to pick at outlet plugs and shove anything from Popsicle sticks to bobby pins into the holes they discover.

And, if there are stairs in the home, block them with a baby gate or keep children away from stairs unless you are helping them go up and down. Most toddlers love stairs!

Preschoolers and School-Age Children

Ask your clients for guidelines about whether you have to be in the room with a preschooler or school-age child at all times. Even if you don't, you need to be aware of what they are doing. If you must leave, check on them often because kids can get into unsafe situations quickly. The younger the child, the more you can use the noise level as a guide. When the child is quiet, investigate.

When children are allowed to play outside, ask about outdoor rules. Most accidents occur when young children are playing outdoors. If the parents don't mention safety rules, establish your own. Preschoolers do best with company because they have adventurous spirits. If an older sister or brother is responsible enough to watch the preschooler while you diaper the baby, limit your time away so that the older sibling doesn't feel like you are taking advantage of him or her.

If youngsters are outside, you should be with them. Before you leave the house, put the key, emergency information, and change for emergency phone calls in your pocket. Then walk through the house to make sure windows and outside doors are shut and locked. If you haven't done so before, try your key in the lock before you close the last door.

Don't count on children remembering outdoor safety rules: such as, don't play in the street, don't chase a ball out of the yard, or don't go to anyone's house without permission. Children often forget safety rules when they're playing and having fun.

When youngsters ride tricycles on sidewalks, you become the traffic controller—especially where the driveway meets the street. Try to find a safe place, such as a schoolyard or park, for children to ride wheeled toys. That way, if the children lose control of the toys, they won't end up in the street. For bicycle safety, children must wear helmets when riding.

If you're allowed to take the children to neighborhood parks, don't let them out of your sight for a second. If they need to use a public bathroom, go with them. Just as a person of the opposite sex can go into a bathroom with a disabled person to help them, you may take children of either sex into the bathroom you prefer. Never let a child go into a public bathroom alone.

When you return home, if anything seems wrong—a door is open or there's a broken window—don't go inside. Instead, go to a neighbor's house or a phone booth and call the police.

Some youngsters are very self-reliant, and some parents give their children more freedom than others. If parents allow a child to do something you're uncomfortable with, say so to the child. "I'm sorry. If you want to ride your bicycle without a helmet, you must wait until your parents get home." Also, if children are allowed to rollerblade or skateboard, make sure they wear safety equipment, such as elbow guards, knee pads, and helmets.

The best way to keep children safe is to be aware of what is going on all the time. If you are watching television or playing video games, the children should be watching or playing right along with you. If the children aren't involved, then you shouldn't get involved. It's best to avoid any activity that distracts your attention from the children. If you're the kind of reader who gets absorbed in a book, leave your book at home. And the only conversation you should concentrate on while babysitting is one with the children. Don't make personal phone calls on the job and don't invite a boyfriend, girlfriend, or other visitors to the house. Babysitting is a big responsibility, and it needs all your attention.

You're Important Too

Your safety is just as important as the children's. Don't forget to take care of yourself and speak up when you need to. You have a right to know if there is a gun in the house and whether it is locked up. If you see a gun that is not locked up, don't touch it or let the children touch it. Leave the house immediately, and take the children with you. Then call your parents or another responsible adult and have them move the gun to a safe place. *Always treat a gun as though it's loaded.*

If a client is abusive to you in any way—verbally, physically, or sexually—do not tolerate this behavior. Even if you think you might have misunderstood his or her intentions, discuss the incident with your parents or another adult whom you trust. Don't let the fear of losing your job or your independence get you fenced into a bad situation.

Always take some form of identification with you when you leave home as well as enough change to make a phone call. Another good idea is to carry the name, address, and phone number of a person to contact in case of an emergency. This information may never be needed, but if it is, you are prepared.

If you are babysitting at night, make sure clients know that you need to be picked up and brought home. On the way home, ask the driver to wait until you have entered your house before driving away. Before you leave home, always make sure that your parents or a trusted adult will be able to pick you up if you need them.

Michaela and her parents have a code sentence that she uses if she feels that she needs their help. "If the children's parents come home drunk or their car doesn't have seat belts, I tell them Mom called and said she had to run an errand in the neighborhood, so she'll pick me up to save them a trip. If they don't believe me, they can even talk to Mom when I call her. Most of the time, they're glad to get out of driving me home."

Remember, your parents want you to be safe—so call them even if you think the reason for doing so might be silly.

Chapter Checklist

✓ Most people respond more calmly if they have considered emergency situations and possible responses beforehand.

✓ Prepare two emergency cards—one for your pocket and one to place beside the telephone.

✓ Write down any special instructions, such as how to call a pager number.

✓ Have your clients walk you through their house, showing you its safety features and describing their safety procedures.

✓ Practice phone safety.

✓ Unless you have specific instructions to do otherwise, do not open the door to anyone you don't know.

✓ Keep doors and windows locked at all times. Know how the door locks work and test them.

✓ Close drapes and blinds when it's dark enough to turn on a light.

✓ Statistics show that 95 percent of child-related accidents can be prevented. So think about safety and prevention.

✓ Do not leave babies or toddlers alone, even for a second. Keep children who are in your care in your sight.

✓ Practice good kitchen and bathroom safety habits.

✓ Keep children away from electrical outlets.

✓ Block stairs and any other unsafe areas.

✓ Establish and enforce outdoor safety rules. Most accidents occur when young children are playing outdoors.

✓ Never let a child go into a public bathroom alone.

✓ When returning to a client's home after an outing, be alert. Open doors or broken windows signal a break-in.

✓ Avoid any activity that distracts your attention from the children in your care.

✓ Consider your personal safety.

✳ Chapter Eleven ✳

First Aid

First aid is emergency care given to an injured or sick person before professional medical care is available. Most of the first aid a babysitter provides comes in the form of hugs, kisses, and Band-Aids. When the situation calls for more extensive first aid, here are some important tips. Remain calm. Take a deep breath. If you have an empty feeling in your stomach or feel confused, you are not alone. But if you stay calm, you will probably be able to think more clearly and make fewer mistakes. Most people make mistakes when they panic.

Doyle and his father were visiting friends. While the adults talked, Doyle pulled an electric coffee pot down, pouring hot coffee on himself. Doyle's dad grabbed his son, rushed to the bathroom, turned on the hot water, and ran it over the child's burns. Doyle's dad didn't even realize his mistake. He should have been using cold water.

One of the virtues of remaining calm is that it rubs off on the child. It's easier to treat calm children. They are more likely to listen and let you handle the situation. One way to insure calmness is to be knowledgeable. The Red Cross gives first-aid classes. In the United States, their phone number is listed in the white pages under American Red Cross. In Canada, it's listed under Canadian Red Cross. Fire departments and hospitals often offer first-aid courses. Taking a first-aid class is the best way to prepare for a medical emergency.

If you do not have first-aid training and cannot take a class, read an up-to-date first-aid book. If you check a book out of the library, make sure it is up to date. Every year people learn new and better ways to treat sickness and injuries. For instance, not many years ago, baby aspirin was used to treat fevers in children. Now aspirin is linked to *Reye's syndrome*, a very serious illness, and is no longer recommended for children.

Another source of first-aid information is the Internet. Ask your doctor or a librarian to suggest some reliable sites. Then print out the information and have a responsible adult review it before you read or memorize it. Keep in mind that Internet sites may have outdated or incorrect information.

No matter where you obtain reliable first-aid information, read it regularly to keep it fresh in your mind. If you know what to do, you will probably remain calm.

Emergency Consent Form

Request that parents fill out an emergency consent form giving you permission to authorize medical care for their children. Most doctors and hospitals won't provide medical care for a child unless the parents have given written consent for the caregiver to obtain treatment. State laws differ, so have your clients find out whether the form has to be *notarized* and filed with their doctor and hospital of choice. Of course, your clients should give you a copy or keep one in their home for you to use if necessary.

PARENT CONSENT FOR TREATMENT

I _____ , hereby give my consent to

   parent's name

_____ to authorize all necessary and

   caregiver's name

appropriate medical treatment for my children. I assume financial responsibility for all necessary care provided. This consent form is in force until canceled in writing.

_____ , _____

child's name   birth date

_____ , _____

child's name   birth date

_____ , _____

parent signature   date

_____

address

_____

city/state/zip

_____

home phone

_____

work phone

_____

cellular phone or pager number

Phoning for Emergency Assistance

To be well prepared for an emergency, write a sample script for yourself. Practice it until it becomes second nature. Practice it with your friends, your parents, or by yourself. Say it out loud, over and over, so that you can hear yourself say the words. Say them into a tape recorder and play them back to see whether your words and meaning are clear.

When you are phoning for emergency help, it is acceptable to reveal that you are the babysitter and give out the name, address, phone number, and personal information about the family you are sitting for. Bear in mind that an emergency is the *only* acceptable time to give anyone this information. Even then, the information must be limited to what is necessary for emergency personnel to do their job.

Consider this emergency situation. You are sitting seven-year-old Tabatha. She scrambled up the backyard tree, fell to the ground, and won't answer you. You can see that she is breathing, but you don't know how badly she is injured. You can't move her because you might cause further injury. So you cover her with your sweater, dash for the phone, and dial the emergency number.

When the operator answers, you say: "My name is _____. I'm the babysitter at __address_____, and the phone number here is _____. Tabatha is seven. She fell out of a tree in the backyard. She's breathing but not moving or responding to my voice. I covered her with my sweater. I had to leave her alone to come inside and make this call."

At this point, the operator may ask you questions or give you instructions. Repeat the instructions to be sure they are correct and clear in your mind. Then follow the instructions. Do not hang up the phone unless you are told to do so.

Waiting during an emergency is probably the most frustrating time because you want to yell, "Just hurry up and get here!" But remember that the emergency team has already been alerted, and anything the operator asks or instructs you to do will benefit you and Tabatha.

Calling for Emergency Help

Always call for emergency help *first,* and call the parent *second* when:

- breathing is difficult or has stopped.
- a wound covers a large area.
- a wound won't stop bleeding.
- a cut is serious.
- a burn covers a large area of the body (such as the whole hand).
- a burn causes the skin to blister, open, and weep.
- a burn appears brown or black.
- an object is in the eye, ear, or nose.
- a bone appears to be broken.
- someone is choking.
- a sharp object has been swallowed.
- there is severe pain or pain lasts longer than a half hour.
- someone is *unconscious.*

- there is a severe allergic reaction to bee sting or insect bite.
- a child ingests a poison.

When first aid is necessary, protect the patient and yourself. Wash your hands before and after giving treatment to minimize the chance of passing germs back and forth. The American Red Cross suggests that you wear latex gloves any time there is bleeding to protect yourself from the transmission of disease. Most health-care professionals wear latex gloves when they treat patients. Your safety is as important as the health-care providers'. Disposable latex gloves are sold in any drugstore. If latex gloves are not available in an emergency situation, use bread bags, plastic food-storage bags, or plastic wrap.

Whenever you are in doubt about what to do in case of sickness or injury, call the children's parents or another responsible adult. If a child is sick or injured while in your care, but not seriously enough to contact a parent, *always* write a note about what occurred—no matter how insignificant it seems to you. Put the note where parents will see it in case you forget to tell them about the incident. A stubbed toe or slight fever may be just that, or it could escalate into something to be concerned about.

Know the location of first-aid supplies, such as Band-Aids, syrup of ipecac (for specific types of poison), fever reliever, medicine spoon or cup, sunscreen, tweezers, and a thermometer. *Never* give or apply any medication to children without specific instructions from the parent, a doctor, a nurse, a poison-control operator, or an emergency medical technician.

Common First-Aid Problems

Here is a brief list of common first-aid problems and treatment suggestions:

Bee Stings

Scrape off the stinger with something flat, such as a fingernail file or the back of a table knife. The flat surface helps to avoid squeezing the sac on the stinger that holds the poison. Wash the area with soap and water. Then place ice cubes in a plastic bag, wrap the bag in a cloth, and hold this cold pack on the injury. The ice helps numb the pain. If ice is not available, a bag of frozen peas, corn, or mixed vegetables wrapped in a cloth works too. *Do not use blue ice or freezer packs because they can cause frostbite.*

If the child develops any unusual symptoms such as nausea, vomiting, or difficult breathing, call 911 or the emergency help number *first*. Then, call the parents *second*. The child may be having an allergic reaction, which can be life-threatening.

Bites

Wash the area with soap and warm water. If teeth have broken the child's skin, call the parent. If there are multiple bites or severe bleeding, call the emergency help number.

Bumps and Bruises

Place an ice-cube pack or a bag of frozen vegetables wrapped in a cloth on the area (see instructions under Bee Stings) for about ten minutes. *Do not use blue ice or a freezer pack*. If the bump is on the head, use the cold pack. Have the child stay quiet, and call the parents for further instructions. Watch the child for unusual symptoms, such as dizziness, vomiting, sleepiness, irritability, differences in the appearance of the eyes, or inability to use arms and legs normally. If any of these symptoms are present, call for emergency help.

Burns

For a minor burn, run *cold* water over the burn for seven to ten minutes. Cold water cools the burn and lessens the pain. For more serious burns or burns that cover large areas, call for emergency help and instructions. Then contact the parent.

Choking

You can use the Heimlich maneuver for older children but not for younger children. In first-aid classes, you will learn proper procedures firsthand—the best way.

If a child puts something in his or her mouth and is coughing, gagging, or choking, then swallows and seems okay, be sure to call the parents and let them know what happened. It is possible for a swallowed object to cause irritation or damage that can lead to an infected windpipe or pneumonia.

Cuts, Punctures, and Scrapes

Whenever there is bleeding, the caregiver should use disposable latex gloves. Good substitutes are bread bags, plastic food-storage bags, or plastic wrap.

Minor Cut
Use a washcloth, soap, and warm water to gently clean the cut. When the wound is clean, pat it dry, and cover it with a Band-Aid.

Major Cut
Cover the wound with a clean cloth, apply pressure to it, elevate it above the heart, and call for emergency help.

Puncture Wound
Apply a washcloth moistened with soap and warm water to the wound. Then call the parent.

Scrape
Gently wash the scrape with soap and warm water. Rinse under warm, running water. When the wound is clean, pat it dry. If the area is too large for a Band-Aid, call the parents. Scrapes and burns are closely related. The larger they are, the more likely they are to need professional attention.

Earache, Toothache, Sore Throat
Keep the child as quiet as possible with distraction techniques, such as soft music, stories, or simple games. If distraction techniques don't work, call the parents or a responsible adult for help. Write down any instructions, repeat them back, and follow them. If the parents do not return home and the child is still uncomfortable after another half an hour, call them again.

Fever

Keep the child quiet. Offer him or her water or juice to offset any moisture lost from sweating. Dress the child in lightweight clothing and cover him or her with a sheet rather than a blanket. Call the parent. Never give any medication without specific instructions, preferably written, from the parent.

Nosebleed

Any time there is bleeding, the caregiver should use disposable latex gloves. Good substitutes are bread bags, plastic food-storage bags, or plastic wrap.

Have the child sit with his or her head bent slightly forward and breathe through the mouth. Either you or the child should pinch the fleshy part of the nose together for five to seven minutes. When the bleeding has stopped, gently clean the child with a washcloth moistened with warm water and soap. Then, keep the child quietly distracted for at least another half hour. Do not let the child blow his or her nose.

If the bleeding has not stopped after ten minutes, call the parent. If the bleeding is caused by an injury to the nose, call for emergency help. Then call the parent.

Poison

If you suspect a child has swallowed something poisonous, investigate calmly. A frightened child will avoid telling the truth to keep from getting into trouble. But time is valuable. As you calmly ask questions, scan the area for clues to identify the poison. Take any suspect plant or container to

120

the phone with you and call the Poison Control Center. Tell the poison-control specialists the age of the child, the name or description of the suspected poison, and the suspected amount that the child swallowed. Follow their directions. Do not give the child any medication or drinks without specific instructions. *All over-the-counter medicines and drugs are a potential poison.*

Splinters

Wash your hands. Wash around the splinter with warm, soapy water. Clean the tweezers with soap and hot water. With the tweezers, hold the splinter close to the entry point and pull it out. When you remove the splinter, soak the injury for about five minutes, and pat it dry. If some of the splinter was left behind, do not try to dig it out. Soak the injury and tell the parents as soon as they come home.

Sprain

Have the child sit or lie on something comfortable. Elevate and ice the sprained area. Always cover an ice-cube pack or bag of frozen vegetables with a cloth or towel. *Do not use blue ice or a freezer pack.* Call the parent.

Stomachache

Make the child comfortable, then check for other symptoms. If the child has a fever, is dizzy, looks pale, or feels nauseated, call the parent. Even if there are no other symptoms, contact the parent if the stomachache lasts more than a half hour. Do not give the child food, drink, or medication unless told to do so by the parent.

121

Common Poisons Found in and Around the House

- Alcohol
- Ammonia
- Antifreeze
- Antihistamines (cold medicines)
- Birth Control Pills and Creams
- Bleach
- Bubble Bath
- Bug Spray
- Button Batteries (in watches, calculators, and cameras)
- Cigarette Butts
- Cleaners
- Cologne and Perfume
- Dandruff Shampoo
- Deodorant, personal and room
- Detergents
- Drain Cleaner
- Fabric Softener
- Fingernail Polish and Remover
- Furniture Polish and Wax
- Gasoline
- Hair-care Products
- House Plants
- Iodine
- Kerosene
- Lighter Fluid
- Lye
- Model Cement
- Mothballs
- Painkillers
- Paint Remover and Thinner
- Paints and Permanent Markers
- Plant, Tree, and Vine Berries
- Prescription Drugs
- Sunscreen
- Toiletries
- Tranquilizers
- Turpentine
- Vitamins
- Weed Killer
- Wild Mushrooms

Chapter Checklist

✓ When emergency first aid is required, try to stay calm. Most people make mistakes when they panic.

✓ Taking a first-aid class is the best way to prepare for an emergency.

✓ If you cannot take a first-aid class, get reliable, up-to-date first-aid information and read it regularly to keep it fresh in your mind.

✓ Request that parents fill out an emergency consent form giving you permission to authorize medical care for their children.

✓ Sometimes a sitter should call for emergency help *first,* and call the parent *second.*

✓ When first aid is necessary, protect the patient and yourself. Wash your hands before and after giving treatment, and wear disposable latex gloves or a substitute for them if the child is bleeding.

✓ Whenever you are in doubt about what to do, call the children's parents or another responsible adult.

✓ Know the location of first-aid supplies, such as Band-Aids, syrup of ipecac (for specific types of poison), fever reliever, medicine spoon or cup, sunscreen, tweezers, and a thermometer.

✓ *Never* give or apply any medication to children without specific instructions from the parent, a doctor, a nurse, a poison-control operator, or an emergency medical technician.

Chapter Twelve

Accidents and Emergencies

It's a cold, windy day. Kenneth's parents say his friend, Andy, can stay and play while they are gone if it's okay with you. You agree.

While you're fixing them lunch, the boys disappear into the front room. Your ears pick up a suspicious sound, and you decide to investigate. You dash out of the kitchen and see Andy's football leave his fingertips just as you say, "No football in the house." Kenneth misses. The ball hits the window and glass shatters everywhere.

What should you do?

a) Make the boys clean up the mess.

b) Leave the mess for the parents, and ask Andy to leave.

c) Clean up the glass while the boys eat.

d) Yell, scream, and stomp.

e) Count to ten, let the boys eat, and then ask them to help you clean up.

If you yell, scream, and stomp, you are out of control and not much of a role model. Having the boys clean up the glass by themselves could turn the accident into a serious emergency. Leaving the mess for the parents and asking Andy to leave might work. But is this the best solution? How cooperative do you think Kenneth will be the next time you sit? Cleaning up while the boys are eating leaves them unsupervised. Look what just happened! And, if you clean up the mess alone, it relieves them of any responsibility for their actions. The best choice is *e*. Count to ten, let the boys eat, and then ask them to help you clean up.

Make sure you and the children have, and keep, your shoes on. If the broken item is electric—for instance a lamp—pull the plug. Don't allow young children to touch any broken glass with their hands, even large pieces. Use a broom and dustpan to sweep up large pieces of glass, and then vacuum thoroughly in case small slivers remain. Put the glass in a garbage receptacle that is safely out of the reach of the children. Tell the parents what happened as soon as they get home. Accidents happen. It won't be the first time, or the last. Remember how embarrassed you were when an accident happened to you. How you wanted the accident to be handled? Try to handle this situation in the same way.

It's likely that you will never have to face an emergency as a babysitter. The first rule in any emergency is to remain calm. When you are calm, you are more likely to act rationally and the children will follow your example. In most cases, if you are prepared with information and practice good safety procedures, you will be able to handle the emergency.

Remember the advice mentioned earlier in this book: Prepare two cards with emergency information, and put one beside the phone and one in your pocket or wallet. You won't have to waste valuable time searching for important phone numbers if you need them.

Common Emergencies

Here is a brief list of common emergencies with suggestions on how to handle them:

Child Abuse

If you suspect child abuse, or if a child says he or she is being abused, remain calm. Listen, but don't take the matter into your own hands. Talk to your parents, a school counselor, or a child-abuse agency about your concerns. Let adults make the ultimate decision about turning in parents to authorities unless a child is obviously in danger. Don't gossip or spread rumors. Child abuse is serious, but false accusations cause tremendous harm. Family reputations can be ruined, and parents and children can be traumatized. There is a child-abuse hotline: 1-800-4-A-CHILD.

Earthquakes

Earthquakes are frightening, but try to remain calm and reassure the children. Most quakes last only for a short time, usually less than thirty seconds, but they seem to last forever. Do not go outside until the shaking has stopped completely and there is no risk of aftershocks. You and the children could be hit by falling bricks and debris, glass, or power lines.

If you are in "earthquake country," you have probably practiced "duck and cover" in school. Always ask parents if they have a home plan and practice it with the children. Or ask school-age children to demonstrate what they've learned about earthquake safety.

If you're not in "earthquake country," you can still have an earthquake. "Duck and cover" is the best method of protection, even in a house. Crouch down under a sturdy table or chair and hold on. The next best strategy is to stand under an interior door frame. Stay as far away from walls, windows, mirrors, shelves, tall pieces of furniture, large appliances, and breakable glass as possible.

When the quake is over, there may be aftershocks. If the phone is working, and you wish to call the children's parents and your parents, keep the call short. If you don't reach either party immediately, don't tie up the phone lines. Wait for them to call you. Stay off the phone so that lines will be free for people with emergencies.

Continue to reassure the children. Do what you can to distract their fears. If you can distract your own fear, you will go a long way toward soothing theirs. Use your imagination.

Don't use the electricity until you know it's safe to do so. If your clients have an emergency kit (see Power Failure), locate it and turn on the portable radio for information and instructions.

Fire

Do not try to put the fire out. If you smell smoke or the smoke alarm goes off, get yourself and the children out of the house immediately. If you see smoke, crawl along the floor until you can get out.

Run to a neighbor's house or a pay phone to call the fire department. Never stop to call from the house. Remember, the most important thing to do is get everyone out of the house quickly.

If you're on the second floor (or higher in an apartment building), do not use the elevator. It could malfunction and trap you and the children. If the stairs are blocked by smoke, go in a room, close the door, and signal at an open window with a sheet or a piece of clothing.

Once you are safely outside, do not go back inside the house for a pet, a special blanket, a toy—or anything else. You could die of smoke inhalation.

Gas Leak

If you smell gas, do not turn lights or anything electrical on or off. The spark could ignite the gas. Don't light any matches. If the source of the gas smell isn't discovered immediately—for instance, a stove burner—leave the house. Go to a neighbor, request help, and call the gas company. When the source is discovered, and the gas leak is eliminated, air out the house until the fumes are gone.

Plumbing Problems

If a pipe or washer hose breaks or a toilet overflows, turn off the water valve if possible. Remove children from the flooded area. If there is more than a small leak, call the parents or a responsible adult to help you. Rising water is a dangerous problem as it can come in contact with electrical wires or extension cords and cause severe electrical shock. Do not put yourself or the children in any danger. Leave the house. Go somewhere safe, and call for help.

Power Failure

If a power failure occurs during the day, pretend you're camping in the woods. What would you do to stay warm? What could you eat that didn't need to be cooked? Play a game of make believe or checkers. Limit how often you open the refrigerator and freezer. If you need to warm a baby bottle, run hot water over it (water in the water heater stays warm for some time) until the milk is the correct temperature.

If it's nighttime, stay calm. Make a game of exploring to find a flashlight. Never use anything with an open flame for light. If the phone is working, call the power company and the children's parents. If you can't find a flashlight, and you can't see the phone number on the emergency card to reach your clients, call your parents or another responsible adult for assistance. Then pile up blankets and pillows, snuggle together, and tell jokes or funny stories until help arrives. Don't allow roughhousing.

If the phone isn't working, keep yourself and the children busy. Ask them if they've ever been to camp and what their favorite activity is when it's dark. Do you know any silly camp songs? Start singing.

If you live in an area where power outages are common, prepare an emergency kit. Include a flashlight, a portable radio, extra batteries for any equipment that requires them, stick lights, a wind-up clock, and a manual can opener.

Prowler

If you feel uneasy or suspicious about a noise outside, do *not* go outside to investigate. Stay calm and call the police. After you report your concerns, give them the family information they will need from the emergency card you keep beside the phone. Usually, the police will keep you on the phone until a patrol car arrives. Do not open the door until you are sure it is the police.

If you actually hear someone trying to break in, grab the children and escape through another door or a window. Go to a neighbor and ask for help. If you can't escape, take the children into a room—preferably one with a phone extension so that you can call for help—and barricade the door with furniture.

Stranger

If you are outside with the children and a person approaches who is not familiar to you or the children, go inside *immediately* and lock the door. If the person does not leave, call the police. Children can also meet strangers on the Internet. Monitor their online activity.

Tornadoes or Hurricanes

If you live in an area of the country where there are tornadoes and hurricanes occur regularly, you probably have experience to draw from. Find out what kind of safety precautions the children's family usually takes and make a game of practicing these safety plans now and then. Do they have an emergency kit (see Power Failure)? If so, grab it on your way to safe places. Which area is the safest place in the house?

Keep in mind that the safest places to take shelter are the interior rooms of the house, an inside hallway, or a basement room. Stay away from windows, mirrors, and any kind of glass that can shatter. Also, ask a trusted adult for additional information that will help keep you and the children safe.

If you have a storm warning, call the parents so that they have the opportunity to return home or give you specific safety instructions if they cannot return home. Stay calm and try to distract yourself and the children with games, songs, and stories.

Chapter Checklist

✓ The first rule in any emergency is to remain calm. When you are calm, you are more likely to act rationally, and the children will follow your example.

✓ If you suspect child abuse, don't take the matter into your own hands. Talk to your parents, a school counselor, or a child-abuse agency about your concerns.

✓ If there is an earthquake, do not go outside. Practice the "duck and cover" method to avoid falling debris or shattering glass.

✓ In case of a fire, get everyone out of the house quickly, staying close to the floor if there is smoke. Go to a neighbor's house or a pay phone to call the fire department.

✓ If you smell gas, do not turn lights or anything electrical on or off, and do not light any matches. Go to a neighbor, request help, and call the gas company.

✓ When plumbing problems happen, turn off the water valve if possible, remove the children from the flooded area, go somewhere safe, and call for help.

✓ During nighttime power failures, try to find a flashlight. Never use anything with an open flame for light. Use distraction techniques to keep the children busy.

✓ If you feel uneasy or suspicious about a noise outside, do *not* go outside to investigate. Stay calm, and call the police.

✓ If you are outside with the children and a stranger approaches, go inside *immediately* and lock the door. If the person does not leave, call the police.

✓ Children can also meet strangers on the Internet. Monitor their online activity.

✓ Keep in mind that the safest places to take shelter during a tornado or hurricane are the interior rooms of the house, an inside hallway, or a basement room. Stay as far away from walls, windows, mirrors, shelves, tall pieces of furniture, large appliances, and breakable glass as possible. If you have a storm warning, call the parents so that they have the opportunity to return home or give you specific safety instructions if they cannot return.

✳ Chapter Thirteen ✳

A Babysitting Kit

What is a babysitting kit? A babysitting kit contains everyday items and activities to entertain children as well as some conveniences for yourself. More important, your babysitting kit is a reflection of the kind of person you are. Have fun with it. Tuck toys into it that you still enjoy. Let the child in you show through your kit. Don't be afraid to tell little children that these are your toys, but you will share them until you go home. Your babysitting kit reinforces the idea of sharing by letting the children know how much fun you are having while you share. Ultimately, the best part of a babysitting kit is not the objects that are in it but you and your imagination. This chapter includes some suggestions to activate your imagination.

Activities for Infants and Babies

Babies are learning from the moment they are born. Tuck things into your kit that encourage a baby to use his or her senses. Sound, sight, and touch are the easiest senses to appeal to at this young age.

To engage a baby's sense of hearing, take along nursery rhymes or songbooks that were your favorites as a child. If you didn't have a favorite, now's the time to find one. Look in the children's section of the library, or ask a librarian for suggestions. Check second-hand bookstores and library sales. Babies also enjoy the sound of a music box, bells, and rattles.

Appealing to a baby's sense of sight sometimes takes more patience and creativity. If you have the time and inclination, you can cut out pieces of paper or aluminum foil and make a mobile with tape, string, and a clothes hanger. (Be sure to place the finished product out of the baby's reach. Doing so not only encourages a child to use his or her muscles but it also keeps little hands from reaching something that doesn't belong in the mouth.) But you don't have to spend hours creating visually stimulating toys. Keep your eyes open for anything that reflects a baby's image. The baby in the mirror fascinates infants.

To activate a baby's sense of touch, gather large pieces of scrap material—velvet, terry cloth, fur, satin—anything that has an interesting texture. If you have the time and like to sew, you might want to make soft little pillows of each material in different, brightly colored shapes.

Although you can't put outdoor activities into your kit, try them for a nice change of pace. If you have the parents' permission and have asked for their directions regarding sunscreen, stroll around the block. Point out neighborhood animals, pretty flowers, and trees. Or take the baby and a blanket into a shady spot in the backyard. Lie down beside the child and let the baby feel the grass. Make sure that nothing ends up in the baby's mouth.

Activities for Toddlers

Toddlers are natural adventurers. They like rhythm, repetition, and noise, and they enjoy copying other's actions. Many of the activities for babies and preschoolers are also appropriate for toddlers.

Toddlers love clapping to music or a favorite nursery rhyme, such as "Hickory, Dickory, Dock." They also like to bang a wooden spoon on pots and pans or boxes. Make up a rhyme with their name in it. They'll love it.

Read-aloud books that have repeated phrases are a tremendous hit with toddlers. Pick books that were your personal favorites or ask a children's librarian for suggestions.

Toddlers enjoy a colorful beach ball to chase and roll around the floor. Sit on the floor and roll the ball to a sitting child. Good luck! But the game is fun even though little ones don't sit still for long. Be sure to set a good example by keeping the ball on the floor—and to be on the safe side—play in a room that has no fragile items around. A long hall or the child's room is the best choice for this game.

Activities for Preschoolers

Children in this age group like make-believe games, songs, stories, books, simple arts and crafts, modeling dough, and puzzles. The secret to any activity involving children is that the more you have fun with it, the more the child will enjoy it. Fun is contagious.

Do you have some favorite song tapes that are appropriate for young children? Bring a tape player and some scarves or large scraps of material and do a veil dance. To stretch their imaginations, make up a story. Get your whole body into it. Do you remember your favorite story when you were little? Use it as a guide and personalize it by using the child's name. Encourage the child to add to the story. Stories don't have to make a lot of sense. In fact, if the child says, "That's not true," congratulate her on how smart she is.

Books are always a good standby. Young children love stories that have colorful characters, bright pictures, and repetition of words or ideas. Do you have a secret desire to be an actor or an actress? Now's your chance. Act out a story and captivate your audience.

Books are also a source of creative ideas for crafts for different age groups. There are craft books at the library on paper folding and paper crafts. Children will be happy learning how to fold or do simple things, so don't start out with anything too complicated. For instance, make a colorful paper hat with the magazine section of the newspaper. Or use folded colored paper and blunt scissors to create snowflakes and other interesting shapes. For a different effect, try tearing instead of cutting. Crayons and coloring books are always a hit, especially if you color right along with the children.

The messier the project, the better children like it. Be sure to include old shirts in your kit to cover their clothes.

Protect the surface you are working on with plastic garbage bags or newspapers and clean up afterward.

Clay or play dough teaches children something about texture and shaping. They love to play with the dough and squish it between their fingers. This activity also relieves stress. You can make modeling dough yourself (see the recipe on this page). Consult with the parent to be sure that the children are not allergic to the ingredients. Since the recipe requires using the stove, make the dough ahead of time at your house.

Paste or glue is another item that comes in handy in a babysitting kit. Bring along some old magazines and cut out objects that the youngster likes. Then make a collage. Or tear out rectangular strips, paste the ends together, and make a paper chain that stretches from one end of the

✳ Recipe for Modeling Dough ✳

In a bowl, mix 1 cup of flour and 1 cup of salt with 2 teaspoons of cream of tartar.

Into a 1 1/2-quart pan, measure 1 cup of water, 2 tablespoons of vegetable oil, and 5 drops of food coloring (the color of your choice).

Gradually stir the dry ingredients into the water mixture.

Cook over medium heat, mixing with a wooden spoon, until the mixture pulls away from the pan.

Let cool. Store in an airtight plastic bag.

house to the other. Glue can also be used to paste a large picture from a magazine onto cardboard. Then cut the reinforced picture into a simple puzzle. Cereal-box fronts make fantastic puzzles too.

A collage can also be made with several food items such as colorful dry beans, pasta shapes like shells (large and small), macaroni, and brown and white rice. Be careful if there are infants or small toddlers present when you use these materials. They can easily find their way into a little one's mouth.

No matter what activity you do with children, you are the teacher. Just because you are older, children will look up to you. If they truly admire you, they will usually copy your excitement as well as the things you do.

A parent put it this way: "The most challenging thing about being a parent is being a good example." If you substitute the word *babysitter* for the word *parent,* this statement still applies.

Activities for the School-Age Child

The older the child, the less you need a physical babysitting kit. Often, by the age of six, children already have favorite things to do. Ask them to show and tell you about their favorite activity. Then listen!

Tony has a business-card collection. Business cards may sound very dull to you, but Tony doesn't feel that way. There's excitement in his voice when he shows off his collection. He speaks of interesting people and unusual professions from several countries of the world. He'd like to work in Asia when he grows up.

Dogs are a favorite for Laura. She's taken her dog through obedience training and dreams of showing him even though he's a mutt. Someday she intends to raise German shepherds.

John is interested in birds. Most of his knowledge came from working at a neighborhood diving-duck preserve. He also has a private library on domestic and exotic feathered friends.

Children don't always share their interests because they think others will be critical, judgmental, or bored. There is nothing more depressing than having someone put down a project you find exciting. So if you're less than enthusiastic about dolls or electronics, listen anyway. Every child is a learning experience.

Children who are hesitant to mention any special interests might enjoy playing a board game, such as Monopoly or checkers. Or create your own game. Make cardboard cards and decorate them, making two of everything. Turn them facedown, mix them, and then try to match them.

Do you want to tickle their funny bone? Or let them tickle yours? Share popular jokes. Riddles and charades appeal to the child with imagination.

Don't be surprised if, at the beginning, you are the children's main interest. It's hard for them to believe that you were ever their age or that they will ever be your age. If you remember how you felt as a child, you will have an advantage because you'll be more sensitive to their needs.

Sometimes children want to talk about sensitive subjects, such as divorce. They may feel that they can't discuss this subject with either parent, but they need to work through the problem by talking about it. Let them talk, but do not take sides and don't tell anyone what a child has told you in confidence unless you suspect child abuse.

Taking an interest in what children like and who they are lets them know that they are important to you. As an older friend who listens, you can help to build their self-worth.

Outside Entertainment

Outdoor play calls for more safety awareness on the sitter's part. Fenced backyards are best, and ask the parents for their guidelines regarding sunscreen.

Who doesn't like soap bubbles? Their rainbow colors and the way they travel in the breeze are fascinating. Bubbles are best blown outside, but some parents allow soap bubbles in the bathroom or kitchen.

Straws make great bubble blowers. Tea strainers, potato mashers, and pancake turners with slots make interesting bubbles. A foil pie tin works well to hold the bubble solution when you and the children are experimenting.

✳ Recipe for Bubble Solution ✳

Any dishwashing liquid makes a good bubble solution.

Into a 1-pint mixing bowl or jar, pour one cup of warm water.

Add 1 tablespoon of light corn syrup and 4 tablespoons of dishwashing liquid.

Mix gently.

Let cool.

Consider putting some simple toys in your babysitting kit. If you're an expert with a yo-yo, you'll have children begging you to show them how to do tricks. And buy a paddleball or two. The ball is attached to the paddle with a length of rubber. It takes some skill, but not a lot, to hit the ball. This game is fun, win or lose. In fact, the less skill you have, the better the youngsters like the game. They catch on fast and contests can last for hours. Jump rope to rhymes or jingles. Bring a couple of jump ropes in case youngsters don't have their own, and trade jingles.

Nature can also provide outside entertainment. Spread a blanket outside, lie back, and find animals in the clouds. Or make a picnic lunch, and then fly a kite. There's no end to the activities you can enjoy by just using some imagination and creativity. Changing items in your babysitting kit from time to time will cultivate interest, yours and theirs.

For the Sitter

You might want to add a few things to your babysitting kit for your own convenience. Bring a flashlight in case the power goes out. A flashlight can also be a game—great for playing finger shadow games. An extra sweater comes in handy when clients keep their house colder than yours. Pencil and paper saves you from having to hunt when you need to take or leave a message

Keep some items in your babysitting kit for emergencies. Latex or plastic disposable gloves are an important addition. You need to avoid direct contact with blood or other bodily fluids. Include important phone numbers: where to reach the children's parents (including cellular phone numbers and pager numbers); who to call if you can't reach the parents; and numbers for the poison center, the police, the fire department, and the children's doctor. Don't forget the first-aid book or information you've gathered. In case your clients haven't left a petty-cash fund for emergencies, carry enough change to make at least two calls from a pay phone.

It's wise to let children know that your babysitting kit is private and that only you can remove things from it. Then keep the babysitting kit out of their reach. This strategy ensures that personal safety items will be available when you need them.

Chapter Checklist

✓ A babysitting kit contains everyday items and activities to entertain your charges as well as some conveniences for yourself.

✓ Ultimately, the best part of a babysitting kit is not the objects that are in it but you and your imagination.

✓ Tuck things into your kit that encourage a baby to use his or her senses.

✓ Toddlers like activities with rhythm, repetition, and noise, and they enjoy copying others' actions.

✓ Preschoolers like make-believe games, songs, stories, books, simple arts and crafts, modeling dough, and puzzles.

✓ The secret to any activity involving children is that the more you have fun with it, the more the child will enjoy it.

✓ No matter what you do with children, you are the teacher. Just because you are older, children will look up to you.

✓ The older the child, the less important a physical babysitting kit is. Often, by the age of six, children already have favorite things to do. Ask them to show and tell you about their favorite activity. Then listen!

✓ Outdoor play dictates more safety awareness on the sitter's part.

✓ Put some items in your babysitting kit for your convenience, such as a flashlight; keep others, such as latex disposable gloves and change for phone calls, for emergencies.

✓ Keep your babysitting kit private and out of the children's reach.

✳ Chapter Fourteen ✳

Smart Sitters

Most babysitters start out sitting for money. But smart sitters continue to sit because sitting is a "giving tree." As in Shel Silverstein's book, what the tree gives depends on the receiver. It may be as simple as acceptance. LeVelle says that with little children, "You are free to be a silly person. They like you just the way you are."

In comparison, you have to gain an older youngster's trust. "It's neat when they accept you like a sister or a friend, confide in you, and ask for advice."

Savvy sitters say that the tree offers self-esteem. "When people trust someone so dear to their hearts with you, it says you are a good person."

The tree gives greater self-confidence. One summer day, Joe took his three charges out into the backyard and sat on a blanket with the baby. A squirrel unexpectedly appeared on the fence. Joe and the children watched it as it chattered and flitted its tail, then raced down the fence, and stopped. Suddenly, the animal dashed at the baby. From that moment, Joe said, every action was in freeze-frame. He reached out, grabbed the squirrel by the tail, hurled the animal over the fence, and rushed the children inside. The baby wasn't hurt, but Joe warned the parents, and they spread the news around the neighborhood. Several days later, the squirrel was captured as it tried to attack another child.

Joe admits that he doesn't know how he responded in the way that he did. From the time he was little, he knew he had been told not to approach or touch wild animals. But somehow, in that split second, he also knew that he couldn't move the baby or the other children to safety in time, but if he was quick, that tail was a handle. Now he has more faith in himself and his ability to deal with the unexpected.

The giving tree, some sitters say, presents opportunities to become a child again, capturing polliwogs and stalking dragons. Children make sitters laugh and help them take themselves less seriously.

Other sitters say they keep sitting because of the independence that the tree provides. They like being their own boss, learning skills in relationships, and forming friendships.

Jennifer and Annette agree that their career choices are directly related to the babysitting giving tree. Jennifer wanted to be a teacher from the time she was in the third grade. Her sitting experience helped her to decide to teach elementary children. She particularly enjoys their active imaginations, their enthusiasm, and their joy of learning.

Annette became a nanny because she likes the way young children burst with natural honesty and curiosity. "They make life an adventure and allow you to continue learning."

Although smart sitters know the tree doesn't offer the same gifts for all, they agree that the babysitting giving tree keeps on giving and giving.

✳ Glossary ✳

antibody—a protein that attacks foreign invaders in the body

asthma—a chronic respiratory disease that is often caused by an allergy. Symptoms include tightness of the chest, coughing, and difficulty in breathing.

baby—a very young child, an infant

babysitting—caring for a child or children when the parents are not at home

bassinet—a bed for a small baby, resembling a basket and sometimes having a hood at one end

colic—severe pain or cramping in the abdomen

CPR—(cardiopulmonary resuscitation) a first-aid procedure used to restore normal breathing and circulation after a person's heart has stopped beating

diabetes—a disorder in which the body produces too little insulin and is unable to control the blood sugar. Symptoms include excessive passage of urine and persistent thirst.

first aid—the emegency care given to an injured or sick person before medical care is available

Heimlich maneuver—an emergency action used to dislodge food from a person's throat to prevent choking

hemophilia—an inherited blood disease that causes the blood not to clot properly and makes bleeding difficult to stop

immune—protected from disease naturally, or by vaccination or inoculation

notarize—to certify a document as authentic by adding the signature of an officer authorized by a court of law

preschooler—a child, usually between the ages of three and five, who is not old enough to attend kindergarten or elementary school

Reye's syndrome—a rare disease characterized by fever, vomiting, and swelling of the brain

savvy—common sense, know-how

seizure—sudden convulsion, involuntary muscle jerks

siblings—people who have a parent in common

strategy—a plan or method to accomplish a specific goal

toddler—a young child who is just learning how to walk

trauma—a severe emotional shock or serious physical injury

unconscious—unable to see, feel, or think

✳ To Find Out More ✳

Books

American Red Cross. *Babysitter's Handbook*. St. Louis, MO: Mosby Lifeline, 1998.

American Red Cross. *First Aid Fast*. Baltimore: StayWell, 1995.

Barkin, Carol and Elizabeth James. *The New Complete Babysitter's Handbook*. New York: Clarion, 1995.

Beecham, Johanna and Ann M. Martin. *Guide to Baby-Sitting*. New York: Scholastic, 1996.

Fletcher, Sarah. *Christian Babysitter's Handbook*. St. Louis, MO: Concordia, 1997.

Guleserian, Mary. *Ultimate Baby-Sitters Survival Guide*. Colorado Springs, CO: Focus on the Family Publishing, 1999.

Kuch, K.D. *The Babysitter's Handbook*. New York: Random House, 1997.

Litvin, Jay and Lee Salk. *Be a Super Sitter*. Lincolnwood, IL: VGM Horizons, 1998.

Pardini, Jane Crowley. *The Babysitter Book*. Chicago: Contemporary Books, 1996.

Smith, Jackie A. and Linda P. Christensen. *Babysitting Basics: A How-To Workbook for Beginning Babysitters*. Salt Lake City, UT: Healthscripts, 1997.

Zakarin, Debra Mostow. *The Ultimate Baby-Sitter's Handbook*. Los Angeles: Price Stern Sloan, 1997.

Videos

Safety Tech: Safe Babysitting. Family Safety, 1997.

Sitting for $uccess: A Video Guide to the Basics of Babysitting. KidKare Productions, 1998.

The Teenager's Guide to Successful Babysitting. Twin Peaks, 1998.

Online Sites

Babysitter Guide to Safety

http://www.stayout.com.babysit.html

Maintained by Guardian Security Services, this site gives tips on choosing jobs wisely, on-the-job safety, emergencies, and getting home safely.

Children's Safety Zone
http://www.sosnet.com/safety/babysitters.tips.html

Provided by the Los Angeles City Fire Department, this site gives guidelines for what to do in case of fire and general babysitting tips.

Healthanswers.com
http://www.healthanswers.com

Partners in this online database include the American Academy of Family Physicians, the Center for Pharmacy, and the National Health Council. In addition to offering a search function for diseases, drugs, injuries, poisons, and symptoms, this comprehensive health site has a Children's Health link that offers children's health subtopics, children's health news, and a children's health library.

Hey Babysitter, Let's Play! Cyber Space Newsletter
http://www.inqpub.com/newsletter.html

Links include Hot Tips, Q & As, Fun and Games, and Crafts and Activities.

✳ Index ✳

✳ About the Author ✳

FRANCES S. DAYEE is the mother of thirteen children and the grandmother of twelve. She has been writing for and about children for more than twenty years, and she has taught writing classes for children and adults. She has also authored two books about child abuse. Ms. Dayee enjoys spending time with children and animals. Her hobbies include camping and reading. She lives in Seattle, Washington.